TO PETER CARVE, O

MAY YE GRANDE

YE X GRANDE

MUCHES GRANDES

Rob Lear

ROB LEAR

ROB

D0472073

Library of Congress Cataloging in Publication Data

Crosbie, Michael J.
  The Jersey Devil design/build book.

  1. Jersey Devil (Firm)   2. Architect-designed
houses——United States.   I. Title.
NA737.J47C76   1985   728 ' .092' 2   84-26367
ISBN 0-87905-190-6

This is a Peregrine Smith Book

Published by Gibbs M. Smith, Inc.
Peregrine Smith Books
P.O. Box 667
Layton, UT 84041

Book design by J. Scott Knudsen

All photographs and drawings have
been published by authority of the
copyright owners.

Cover photograph by Steve Badanes:
The Hill House in the setting sun.

Printed in Japan.

The Jersey Devil
Design/Build Book

Michael J. Crosbie

➔P

Gibbs M. Smith, Inc.

Peregrine Smith Books

For the folks,
Leo and Vi,
and Sharon.

Contents

Foreword

"All artists are close to madness; it is their art that keeps them sane." John Flannagan, Sculptor

When Mike Crosbie asked me to write the foreword to this book I was both honored and intimidated, two states of mind I seldom experience. His request implied that because I had lived through and recorded some of the formative years of this group of architects that I was qualified to make profound judgements concerning the meaning of their work. I am not.

Mike Crosbie has chosen to add a chapter in the history of a most curious group of creators at a no less curious time in architectural history, Orwell's 1984. They were part of a movement that was lumped together under the heading of the "Counter Culture" inspired by Theodore Roszak's book, *The Making of a Counter Culture*. The idea is probably no more misleading than the term "Modern Movement," which was a literary device to aggregate a number of architects that individually had little relation to and often little sympathy for each other.

All the architectural contradictions apparent in today's world were apparent and widely discussed by the mid-1960s. The magazine *Progressive Architecture*, under its then-editor Jan Rowen, published every one of them. Being an editor and eventually the editor in chief of *PA*, I know that we took an interest in the activities of young architects during this time. Another editor, C. Ray Smith, was more sensitive to their activities than the rest of us. His article on Prickly Mountain in the May 1966 issue, describing Yale architecture students building and entrepreneuring in a Vermont ski area, introduced this particular architecture phenomenon to the rest of us. These architects brought a feeling of excitement, adventure, and life to architecture in the 1960s no less essential to it then than now.

Mine is not an intellectual conviction that what these young architects did (or do) is right. Their work did and still does appeal to me. In my opinion it is in the best architectural tradition of America as an industrial democracy described so well by John Kouwenhoven in his books, particularly *The Arts in Modern American Civilization*. They and I share a conviction that architecture is an extension of our lives, not that we give our lives to art as did proper Victorians and Renaissance artists. One such artist, Benvenito Chellini, bragged that his skill as a goldsmith exempted him from common morals, and he lived accordingly. Jersey Devil says the opposite. To them architecture is a means of aiding people in the painful task of making themselves comfortable in this world and a personal way of improving human relations and their own lives. Their architecture has become so much a part of them that they can say, like the Balinese, "We have no art, we do the best we can."

Some of us had hoped two decades ago, as did Jersey Devil, the young men at Prickly Mountain, Ant Farm, Zomeworks, Farallones Group, and the communes scattered from California to Colorado, that if the right alternatives could be found we might be able to skip Orwell's 1984 as some buildings superstitiously jump from the 12th to the 14th floor. We were not successful. I remain convinced, however, two decades later, that an alternative was offered then, as Mike has written here, that remains and is perhaps more viable today.

But strangely enough, in a paradoxical way, their ideas did have consequence. The architect as developer, which twenty years ago was unheard of, is an "ethic" that traces its roots back to the curious combination of ideas discussed in the sixties to realize your art through making money, to realize your intellectual potential by working with your hands, that the building grew as a living thing through collaboration of head and hand instead of springing as a full-blown concept from the designer's mind. This harked back to the old craftsman's motto: "By head and hand all arts do stand," adopting the preindustrial revolution motto of craftsmen as a preface to the information revolution. The contradiction at Prickly Mountain was of affluent youths dreaming of inventing architecture for the poor; using the building of second homes and ski lodges as their prototypes was not without irony. Jersey Devil uses the solar spine of a surgeon's house as the possible solution for factory solar heating in a reversal of Corbusier's adoption of grain silos to domestic architecture.

To me, the "Woodstock" of counter-culture architects took place in Freestone, California, in March of 1970. I published the proceedings in an article titled "Advertisements for a Counter Culture" in the July issue of *PA*. I gave one page of the magazine to each participating group and asked them to write their own unedited "advertisement" as we permitted any commercial advertiser. The traditional architectural community did not greet that issue with overwhelming enthusiasm. Excerpts from my editorial of the issue might be of interest as a historical note on the Zeitgeist of the time:

". . . The purpose of the gathering was stated by Sim Van der Ryn in the invitation 'to learn to design new social forms, new building forms, that are in harmony with life . . . to build a floating university around the design of our lives.'

"Counter culture, opinions, alternatives, change—call it what you will—an increasing number of architects, planners, designers, teachers, artists, are searching for dimensions of their professions outside of what they feel are the narrow limits imposed by an increasingly restrictive society.

FORREST WILSON
WASHINGTON, D.C.
JANUARY 1985

"Protest today is not, as in the past, restricted to demands for economic advantage or political power. It centers, instead, around the demand for other relations among men and it strikes at the very root ideas from which our society grows. It is often unorganized, anarchistic, and irrational. The chief protesters, the revolutionary young, must mature before their priorities fall into place and clearly defined social goals develop. Yet, despite the chaos and confusion sparked by these restive youths, there are many who agree with Theodore Roszak when he says, 'I am at a loss to know where, besides among these dissenting young and their heirs of the next few generations, the radical discontent and innovation can be found that might transform this disoriented civilization into something a human being can identify as home. They are the matrix in which an alternative, but still excessively fragile future, is taking shape.'

"The following pages reflect deep discontent with things as they are. We should be concerned when such options cease to be advertised, for it is when those who seek change despair of its realization that violence becomes inevitable. The public notices that follow are put forth to offer alternatives to our way of life, not to destroy it.

"But what has happened in this period of protest to that part of architecture that is fine art? Here are the architects who, fascinated with technological innovation, are profoundly distrustful of its prevailing goals. They see technology as a device to expand man's consciousness rather than simply a means of increasing his material well being. For example, the pneumatically tensed membrane becomes an 'air pillow' put to uses Frei Otto and Victor Lundy would never have dreamed, and Buckminster Fuller's geodesic dome becomes a Zomeworks climb toy. At the Freestone Conference, technology became the stuff of fine art.

"Whatever is important in the fine arts, in this era of protest, has been bequeathed to architecture. As André Fermigier, the French art critic, wrote in September 1968 following the French student upheavals, 'There is doubtless little hope nowadays for painting, in view of what has become of it in the past few years. Perhaps painters will arise in the future, meanwhile all we can do is entrust art into the hands of architecture, which can still say all that is to be said if it avails itself to the means. . . .' "

I must confess that I do not think a great deal differently today than I did then, fifteen years ago. I would change very little of what was said in that editorial. This means that I either have a very hard head, am slow to learn, or just possibly we may have been right.

Introduction

Steve Badanes with Donna Walter and Floyd Bite. *Photo: Michael J. Crosbie.*

It is a bright June morning in suburban Virginia, just beyond the Washington Beltway. As my car climbs a rocky, winding driveway, the sound of Skil saws pierce the air. A little closer, one can hear scrap pieces of lumber drop, the layered rhythm of pounding hammers, garbled shouts. This is the site of Jersey Devil's current project, a huge residence (affectionately called the Hoagie House) on a densely wooded seven acres on the highest spot in Fairfax County. The project is big by any standard: 9,000 square feet comprised of a main house, a guest house, and a gate house—the largest and most extravagant piece of Jersey Devil architecture in the group's dozen-year history.

Jersey Devil (named for a winged and cloven-hoofed character of mythic proportion that roams the environs of southern New Jersey) is made up of four architects: Steve Badanes, John Ringel, Jim Adamson, and Greg Torchio. If there is a fifth devil (like a fifth Beatle) it is Donna Walter, Steve's sidekick. Around this core revolves a collection of friends and acquaintances from across the country who have participated over the years in the creation of Jersey Devil projects. For this is no ordinary architecture firm, as the architecture surely shows, but a traveling band of "architects, artists, craftsmen, and inventors," as Jersey Devil describes itself, "committed to the interdependence of building and design."

Jersey Devil is unlike most firms in that the architects physically build what they design. Some architects will occasionally act as their own developers or general contractors, coordinating building construction, but the Jersey

John Ringel. *Photo: Michael J. Crosbie.*

To Rob—
Xmas '93
APACHE CREEK
Santa Fe NM.
xxx
SBadanes
12/25/93

Devil architects are a few of only a handful in America today who actually put on the tool belts, swing the hammers, and give life to their own designs. Their personal involvement in the construction of their projects has resulted in an architecture that evolves much like a piece of sculpture or a new invention, where the creator constantly reviews, reconsiders, and adjusts to meet new insights and circumstances. This process is enhanced by the fact that Jersey Devil often lives on the building site during construction, committing to a total involvement with their work. Few architects today seem willing to make such a commitment to their own architecture.

This was not always the case. Much of early America was built by architects who operated similarly to Jersey Devil. They were called "architect builders" and often traveled through a region designing and building houses, churches, stores, and schools. They too would begin with some basic assumptions about the building required, develop designs, and then execute them, making adjustments to meet the demands of site, materials, program, and climate.

It was during the Industrial Revolution that this relationship between architect and architecture began to disintegrate. Mechanized production, the division of labor, and the sheer demand to build more structures faster affected architecture by forcing a wedge between designer and builder. Architects set themselves apart as a professional class that was quite different than mere tradesmen. Buildings were (and still are) designed in their entirety down to the last detail before ground was broken. Then drawn and written instructions were given to the people who would assemble the structure—the builders—who were required by law not to deviate from the plans in any way without expressed permission from the architect. Any changes necessary were communicated back from the building site to the architect in the office.

This divorce was ultimately institutionalized by the American Institute of Architects, which, in 1909, adopted a code of ethics that explicitly forbade architects from engaging in building construction. Thus the hand and the mind were severed in the creation of the built environment. Certain trends in architecture today reflect the malignancy of this separation. Technological advancement is bittersweet: it often makes our lives easier by placing buffers between us and the real world of raw experience. The fabrication of built reality for the architect is not unlike eating synthetic food or engaging in telephone sex. Meanwhile, the ethics of architects who choose to build their own designs are suspect while others receive public acclaim for their unbuilt (if not unbuildable) designs. We live in strange times.

Jersey Devil attempts to rectify this tenuous relationship between architect and builder, design and fabrication, by reuniting the roles. Here, the line between thinking and making becomes indistinct. Design is advanced through the experience of building, which itself is modified as it becomes built reality. Interestingly enough, it is modern building technology that has facilitated this process. Industrialized, prefabricated building materials and automated

Jim Adamson. *Photo: Michael J. Crosbie.*

Greg Torchio. *Photo: Michael J. Crosbie.*

tools have allowed Jersey Devil to build faster and more conveniently. Such materials have also provided an opportunity for reinterpretation of use. Creativity extends into the architects' devising new and unusual ways of using them.

The symbiotic relationship between architect and builder has caused Jersey Devil to draw from the craft tradition for inspiration. While many architects today choose to refer to the "high art" of ancient European architecture, Jersey Devil seeks to connect with the traditions of vernacular, often anonymous folk architecture, the uncelebrated buildings of American culture—anything from rural farm buildings to early industrial structures. Part of that tradition is the use of nonstandard materials and artifacts not intended for building. Incorporated into the design, these humble objects—bottles, blinkers, hubcaps, and headlights—are exalted. The architecture becomes a frame in which an unexpected material is proudly displayed, an everyday object celebrated. Jersey Devil occasionally will include similar materials, although the effect is more polished. Vernacular architecture is also emulated in its handcrafted detail, energy conservation, comfortable human scale, and humor. The light-heartedness of Jersey Devil's architecture reveals the joy (and sometimes the frustration) of creation. The jokes are not private, between the architects and at the user's expense, but engage those who live there and those just passing through. Humor also reflects the function of architecture, both object and the process of making it, as a means for enjoying life: form follows fun.

Jersey Devil's process has its drawbacks. It's not always an inexpensive or quick way to build. Constructing each project "one at a time, one of a kind," as Greg says, also limits the quantity of work that can be produced. And there are restrictions on the size of the projects, which is why most of the work to date has been residential. But these aren't drawbacks for Jersey Devil, because the quality of the work and the joy of building might otherwise be lost.

The bulk of this book is a presentation of Jersey Devil's architecture. The section that follows, however, is important in understanding the architecture. It explains the birth of Jersey Devil, the connection between design and building, the aspect of living on the site, the use of materials, sources of inspiration, and the posterity of what Jersey Devil has wrought. It is explained by those who live it—Steve, John, Jim, and Greg.

A Conversation With Jersey Devil

BEGINNINGS

Jersey Devil's story begins at Princeton University's school of architecture in the late 1960s. It was there that three of the partners met and shared a sense of frustration with their education. Greg, who is ten years their junior, graduated from Ball State University's college of architecture and planning. The four architects speak within the context of their current project, the Hoagie House.

Steve: I went to architecture school without really knowing whether I was going to be an architect or not. I was twenty-five years old, I'd flunked out of college a couple of times. The idea of architecture school wasn't that appetizing to me. But I liked carpentry and art and felt that architecture might incorporate aspects of both, so I figured I'd give it a try. At Princeton the first-year class went down to Dean Geddes's architectural office and the professor said, "This is what architects do, this is where you guys are going to be after school." They didn't say that this was the only option, but that doesn't matter. It's up to each individual to decide what to do with their educational experience. Christmas vacation, I went up to Prickly Mountain in Vermont and people up there were building their own designs, basically using architecture as a way to have a good life. That vision kept me going through three years of school.

John: I went through the school of engineering at Brown University, and it was just numbers. It was mechanical, ungrounded in humanity. So I switched over to architecture [at Princeton] with the mistaken belief that architecture is like engineering in that you build things, which I like to do, but is unlike engineering in that people are the primary concern. Unfortunately, that was not the issue at Princeton. There wasn't really any humanism, there was formalism, and the point of architecture at school was that things match up to certain precepts, which I could handle, being an engineer, because they broke down to formal rules. It was big at that time, you know, regulating lines, all the rehashed Corbusian stuff. The person who was big there was Michael Graves, and of course he's gone through a whole bunch of evolutions since then, and what used to be absolutely unshakeable is now "shakeable." So there I was, dealing with these formalistic precepts that had nothing to do with anything humanistic.

So, I quit school, and Steve and I picked up with playgrounds, which were our first projects, and the first clients were kids. And kids, of course, are pretty straightforward in their reactions to things; either it's boring or it's fun. If it's fun, it elicits reactions like laughter and climbing. And that's it. It's really simple. You don't end up in a discussion of whether the lines are golden means or any other, in my opinion, artificial criteria. You end up with, "Hey! Look at me!" The Arthurpod was a microcosm of that. We shop-fabricated that thing, took it out to the site on a truck, got a bunch of people to help us pick up the various components, cast the footings, and came back the next day and started to assemble it. This entailed putting up the legs, putting the playhouse on top of the legs, and then hanging the slide and swings. Well, we couldn't get it up before the kids from all over the neighborhood were in it and on it and on top of it. We're trying to tie up the tire swing and they'd be trying to swing from it, and we're trying to put up the slide and they're in the playhouse on top waiting for it. So they were having a good time, at which point one of the next door neighbors came over, one of the parents, and told her kids to get off *that thing*. [Laughs] Because she couldn't believe that she was looking at this *thing* in her neighborhood. That *thing* wasn't going to stay *there*, was it? And you kids get over here right now! So

The finished Arthurpod.
Photo: Steve Badanes.

there she was, not being able to see her kids having a good time. All she could see was something that didn't match her formal precepts, whatever they might be. That's what I remember about architectural principles and the Arthurpod. If the kids were up there and having a good time, then we must have done something right. Play is part of humanism.

Steve: We knew Jim the same time at Princeton. John and I both started school without the benefit of an undergraduate

architecture degree, so we had to go three years. They put us in the same class with the juniors, who were architecture majors, and that's where Jim was.

Jim: There was a lot of individual expression going on in the late 1960s while we were in school. There was a lot of rebellion about Vietnam. I think my dissatisfaction with school was due to the lack of relevancy and being uninspired by what the school considered to be good architecture. But there were groups doing innovative work, such as the guys at Prickly Mountain, who were doing a lot of interesting designs and then actually building them. I went up to Vermont after graduation and built a speculative ski house. Going up there was a combination of things: My brother had just bought some land and a friend of ours wanted to invest in something, and I had just gotten out of school with another guy, Jim Proud. We figured we had the perfect combination: land, money, and two talented architects who didn't know shit. [Laughs] Designing and building a house was good experience. We lost money but we learned a lot in the process. I think I satisfied my need to understand what it was like to build something.

John: Steve was the ramrod in those days. He got the projects and he offered work, and I said yes on various different projects, as did other people. So Jersey Devil naturally evolved from those associations with different people on different projects. There was always anarchy. It's a little more formalized now than it ever was, and it's too formalized in a lot of ways. In the original association, if you worked for us, you were a "Jersey Devil." People are out there today, doing many other things,

who used to work for Jersey Devil. We're still project oriented. First there will be us, then there will be a job, then people will come work on it. There will be local people involved in the job. It's not like we're a company and we employ so many people. It's more like an association of individual entrepreneurs who get together because the particular project's too big or too exciting to do it alone.

Greg: I shared some of that excitement, coming from the outside, of first seeing some of their projects. In *Domus* I saw a little thing on the Silo House one time and I said, "Hey, this is great!" Jersey Devil Design/Build. That's all it said. I also admired the name, since my childhood fears were of the legendary devil. I was really glad to see that there was someone doing what I really wanted to do. It gave me some hope, because I was in my third year of architecture school, about 1978.

Steve came to our school in my senior year and was deposited at my desk by one of my professors, because he thought what I was doing was close to Jersey Devil architecture. Steve and I started talking about Jersey Devil, I went to his lecture that night, and we got together afterwards and seemed to hit it off. As we talked he found out that I had a lot of experience in construction; my dad's a builder and I'd been working for him since I was eleven or twelve. While I was in school I had a couple of jobs going, houses I had designed, and I was working on them, doing construction management, doing the drafting, making some money on the side.

Steve told me to look up John in New Jersey, that he could use somebody to do some drafting. I really wanted to work in design/build, but I wanted to get some business experience too. That's still a bit of a joke around here, because if John had no experience in anything, it was business. The day I met him he hadn't made a penny on anything and didn't really think that was important. He couldn't offer me any work, although he had a few jobs that might come through. So I said I had these two jobs lined up on my own and *I* could use

some help. I set up an office in my basement and started working. Little by little he came in more and more and pretty soon he moved into the office with all his stuff, and the Hot Tub House was the first job we did together.

My frame of reference is a lot different from Steve's, John's, or Jim's. There's ten years between us. I guess I'm a lot more practical. I'd like to think that I'm the one they can depend on to get things done, sort of a production

person, relative to them. It's flowing okay and everybody seems comfortable with their roles.

John: On smaller projects, each of us is capable of doing everything. And you'd get a different product from each person. We each have our own particular way of doing things. When we work together there is a give-and-take kind of argument that, to a point, is very productive.

But then somebody's got to decide that they don't care to argue anymore. You can only argue back and forth on issues until you say, "All right, let's do it that way." There aren't too many compromises in the image of the Hoagie House project. Either it looks like a hoagie or it doesn't, and that image develops from the give-and-take argument.

Study model of Hoagie House. *Photo: Steve Badanes.*

When it comes down to more particular things, there is always that same give-and-take. You hammer it out. We all participate in that at all levels. But we have specialties as well. Steve is always there with his crystallizing contrariness. Greg does the drawings; he's definitely the best pencil. I do administration. Jim is noted as the craftsman; if it needs to be framed to within ¹/₆₄th of an inch, he's the man to get on the case.

Steve: John's a genius, but he turns off the design part of himself sometimes. Like Greg says, John gives you the best critique. "He always says what you don't want to hear." John sees things really clearly. He can get this burst of Truth. A lot of us often cloud things up and we don't get it. John gets it.

LIVING

Steve: The thing that makes us different from most architects is a total involvement—we design it, live on the site, and build it. Living on the site is important to me because I love it out here. On a personal level it's important. But I don't do it every time. When we went to Colorado to build the Airplane House, the site was mighty desertlike, so Donna and I rented a house in the mountains with a stream in the yard and snow caps for a view.

I like the idea of not having to commute. I guess living on the site is a romantic notion about how to do it. It's not critical, but it's the old Jersey Devil way.

Jim: Camping out on the site was something that always intrigued me about the projects that Steve and John were working on. When I first started working for them on the Silo House, I lived out of my bus. Owen Hooley was also living on the site in an old army tent. We

Rebar work for the cantilever deck for the Hoagie House. *Photo: Michael J. Crosbie.*

improved our accommodations by building the Cardboard Grotto—we just took saplings out in the woods and bent them over and covered them with cardboard from the shipment of Andersen windows used in the house. It was really quite nice and became the center of the daily "lunch club"; a dozen or so people sitting around a campfire cooking lunch in the woods. This is where you realized it wasn't a normal job site.

John: Over the years, we've always been campers. Anyone who is a camper can appreciate the closeness to your surroundings that camping out brings. We've "camped out" in unheated lofts and "camped in" in unheated cabins. It makes you more aware of the amenities, heat, plumbing, roofs. More grateful, more capable of cutting through the gizmos in your design and relating to basics. Currently I'm not a full-time camper. I've got two little kids and Eve and I feel the "place" of a real house is important to little kids. When they get older, though, we'll move around. That will be part of their education.

Steve: We've had fun doing this stuff. I think if you take that as a significant goal, which I think most people have in their lives, architecture becomes secondary. It becomes a means to a good life. What I *really* like to do is what we're doing right here—be on the site, make your whole life out of this thing, just put down your tools and eat some watermelon. Being able to travel to all different parts of the country, that makes it worthwhile, and you learn something from that too. There's more to it than that, of course, there's a certain serious side, but the important thing is to have a good life. The second most important part is to be a good architect and do something socially responsible.

Jim in his Cardboard Grotto. *Photo: Steve Badanes.*

Site-living at the Football House.
Photo: Steve Badanes.

The lifestyle appeals to a lot of people. When I give a talk to a bunch of people who are older, a lot of them are attracted to the lifestyle. But I think it's the images, the buildings, that appeal to most people.

Greg: I've never had the opportunity to live on the site of a Jersey Devil job and experience the advantage of being totally immersed in the project. My wife, Barbara, and my kids, Giovanna and Greson, allow me the necessary relief from "work."

Our time together as a family and our health are positive forces in my work. These two parts of my life are physically separate, but are strongly influenced by each other.

Jim: When I first arrived on the Hill House job, I found a spot under some oak trees and pitched my tent. I was quite happy until a storm knocked it flat and got me sopping wet. I ended up renting a place for the winter, and the following spring I built myself an alternative structure on the site. I think that was as much a part of the experience as building the house. I wanted it to be free form because I'd never done anything like that before. And I used a method that, I have since found out, Bernard Maybeck used at the turn of the century. I made an armature out of ⅜-inch rebar and then put chicken wire over it. Then I dipped burlap bags into a wet slurry of mortar and spread them over the form. When the cement dried it was strong enough to support a durable layer of trowelled mortar. Very labor intensive, but a very inexpensive way to enclose that space. It was called the Sphincter House, a very appropriate name with its organic openings. I lived in that for a whole year and it was very comfortable.

Completed Sphincter House. *Photo: Steve Badanes.*

There were a lot of people who came from afar to work on the Hill House—part of Steve's network. They would come and camp out on the site. The property was large enough so that each person could pick out a nice, tranquil spot and build themselves a structure, until the first winter storm came and knocked them down. It was fun because we lived there, it wasn't just a job we commuted to. And in the process we got to understand the site a lot better.

DESIGNING

Steve: A building has a life of its own. The typical architect sits at his board, draws his design, wraps up the plans, sends them out for bid, and then some other guy builds it. The design stops right there. But if you're out on the site and you start to frame, say, the joists on this building [points over his shoulder], if they begin to relate to something on the site like this tree, then you might stick a whole bunch more of them out there and see what that does. When you do that with framing, of course you can get into a lot of trouble. Every time you frame something you've got six more processes to go through—insulation, sheetrock, and so on. But it's like a sculptor working with his materials. So if you keep the design really open, you can come up with something truly appropriate. It's like those guys who built the big cathedrals. The architect was there every day and he interacted with the craftsmen who were making it. He was able to see his building grow and work out problems on the site. He didn't have eight million buildings he was flying around to, and he didn't have this incredible bidding and financing process that you have now where everything has to be locked up before ground is broken.

Greg: When we're designing something we start coming up with images and thinking about what it could be. We might end up with something totally different because we search out alternatives. Our first thought is, "How do you build it?" I'd like to think all architects do that. My father taught me never design something you can't build. I may have to learn how to build it, but I'm sure I can build it before it's finished.

Jim: It's important sometimes to step back from the task at hand and see things from a different perspective. One of us will take another's sketch of an elevation and turn it sideways or upside down, and all of a sudden in its new orientation it visually works that way too. It generates a whole new direction of thinking. It's also important to have the capability of not taking things too seriously. There's a very

interesting trademark logo stamped on the lumber we're using right now. It's got a couple of swirling, intersecting curves, and it has the flavor of the type of work that we're doing, especially the Guest House.

Logo on the Guest House's framing lumber.
Photo: Michael J. Crosbie.

The Guest House tower under construction.
Photo: Michael J. Crosbie.

John: Design, in my opinion, is a universal process. It's not necessarily self-conscious. Any time you manipulate something physically, whether you're doing it haphazardly, badly, or well, it's design. It's in the working of it, in the creation of it. Anyone who's putting things together is a designer. Actually putting it together is the important part to me. It facilitates the concept. It ameliorates it, improves it. I think you bring two things to a design—a set of intentions and a preconceived product. The intentions are much more immutable. Intentions, such as permanence, handcrafted, site specific, energy efficient. These can be achieved in numerous final products. In a way, the final product is the frivolous part. The intentions are what you stay attached to, they're your guidelines. The final product works if the intentions show through.

Steve: In school the client was usually portrayed as an ignorant patron. It's a mistake to think that you're going to get good architecture if you just do it and hoodwink the client. To me there's got to be a match between the people and the building. Everything starts with their life—their favorite colors, how they like to eat. You've got to give them a little bit more than they want, you have to make the building continuously be a source of amazement to them. Mystery, discovery, and adventure. But you also have to solve all the basic problems, otherwise they're not going to be able to live in it. I don't try to convince them to build the house, but I try to convince them to build in certain ways once they're committed. I'll fight like hell, sometimes, if I think it's right.

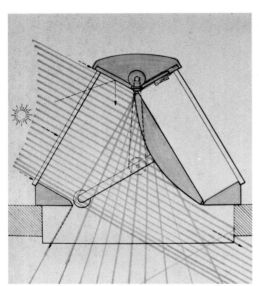

Position of patented Roto-Lid on winter day. *Drawing by Jim Adamson and Greg Torchio.*

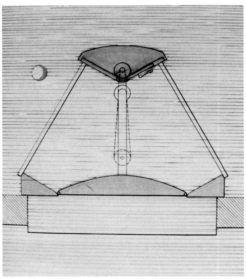

Roto-Lid position on winter night. *Drawing by Jim Adamson and Greg Torchio.*

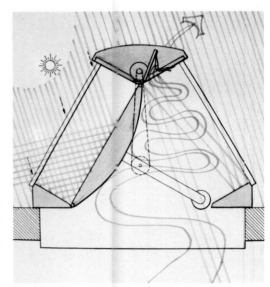

Roto-Lid position on summer day. *Drawing by Jim Adamson and Greg Torchio.*

Jim: Designing a light fixture, say, has a lot to do with intuitively envisioning the quality and effect of light you want. I enjoy making my own fixtures because I get depressed looking at the ones available in the lighting catalogues. One of my favorite pastimes is just walking through hardware stores, looking at the various objects, putting components together, seeing the possibilities of using various materials. Some of them succeed, others don't.

I got involved in a grant to develop an energy efficient skylight. The genesis for this was a design project that never came through. It was a large warehouse/office that required solar heating and daylighting and we realized that the best way to do this was through skylights. I came up with the idea of having an insulated panel that rotates to allow sunlight to enter during the day but at night it rotates to close off the opening and provides an effective means of insulation. During the summer the panel is in a position to block the south sun but allows diffuse north light to enter for daylighting. I call it the Roto-Lid. It's a simple mechanical concept that effectively turns a skylight into an energy efficient device for solar heating and year-round daylighting.

Steve: Greg can flash out eight design schemes in the time you can come up with one. And they'll all be pretty good. He'll do a diagonal scheme, a linear scheme, a circular scheme. He can give you whatever you want and they're all pretty damn good. You begin to wonder though [laughs] because they're all facile as hell. Every once in a while he'll hit one and it's really strong. That's his conceptual way of organizing things. A lot of architects, it looks to me, have

Patented prototype Roto-Lid ready for installation. *Photo: Michael J. Crosbie.*

no way of doing that, no way to start. But when you try to make the building thermally comfortable, you have an awful lot of things to start with. You've got orientation set up, you've got wind protection, views, sun, where you want to approach, where you want to do certain things on the site. If you're always considering design in terms of what it's going to be like if you do things—is the guy going to be comfortable or is he going to be fighting a 60-mile-an-hour wind if he goes out to get a log—the house starts to design itself.

BUILDING

Jim: When I first moved to Vermont to build a house from scratch, none of us were experienced in construction. I didn't think it was possible to do it, to learn all that, to be able to actually build a house that you could live in and have it function. It was a revelation to me to know that it was easily understandable, that it was just a matter of commitment. I think what has happened is that I gained the confidence that I can do things, anything that you want to do as long as you commit yourself to doing it. Not just in building. And it's always important to strive to do that which you don't know how, to experiment. In many cases decisions are made in the design process to use materials or do something that we've never done before just to make it part of our experience.

John: What we all share is a three-dimensional component, something real in the solutions. The problem requires not so much a hands-on solution, but a hands-on understanding of the problem. So certain things you work out on paper. But that's only two dimensional. It's only when the thing is built and all its

horrific implications are staring you in the face in three dimensions that you realize things like "the plumbing pipe is intersecting with the rebar, and that's all sitting under the column." Nothing but the final solution deals with all the components in three dimensions, and we just choose to accept 3-D.

Jim: It's easier to let a space determine itself while you're building it. You get an enclosure or at least a definition of what you're dealing with and then

things start jumping out at you. "That would be great if we did this!" And there are times when we'll knock something down that we've already put up and do something different, because it cries out for something different.

Those sorts of decisions can't be made in the conventional practice where the architect designs something and the builder constructs it according to what the architect has drawn. Whereas we have the advantage of on-site modification that will

Jim working on the Gate House. *Photo: Donna Walter.*

hopefully enhance the end product. There's something very gratifying in building because you get immediate feedback. There are some occupations where you work and never see the product of your efforts. And I suppose satisfaction comes primarily from your position and the money you make. But with designing and building it's really personal. It's using your head and using your hands and creating something that you can look at and sit back and grasp. That's what I still get a kick out of, I really enjoy that. I think that's true for all of us.

Steve: I'd like to see more students know about design/build. I think they'd be having more fun. I know now that architects today aren't very well respected by people who build. In the Middle Ages, as I said about the people who built the big cathedrals, there was a mutual respect between the person who designed the building and the person who made it. Now the architect rarely visits the site, or he won't even go to the site because he won't take the legal responsibility. I think that's all crucial, and we're getting a poor environment because of it, and real bad craftsmanship, because the architect has a low opinion of the maker, and the maker has a low opinion of the architect. If the architect and the maker are the same person, it's got to be different.

Jim: We have had (and I credit Steve for this) real fortune in having excellent clients in all our projects. They've given us basically free rein to do whatever we want within certain constraints. And they usually give us the benefit of the doubt in getting there. A good case in point is the snout on the Hill House. We had a good idea of how we wanted it to look, but how we were going to build it was an on-site mystery. We began by cantilevering 2 × 4s from the roof structure and had them projecting out in free air towards the center of the courtyard. They were flexing up and down in the wind when the client stopped by. He scratched his head and said, "What are you guys *doing*?" We were embarrassed, as if we had been caught. But he came back a few days later and was impressed by what we had done, so it turned out all right. But that's the type of client you need, somebody who's willing to give the freedom to do interesting work.

Greg: I just love working outside, coming out here to the site to work, driving a bulldozer. There's probably something in the AIA code of ethics about architects making money driving bulldozers—one boyhood dream when you were there in the sandbox pushing trucks around. That's something I always wanted to do and now I've got the opportunity to do it. I'm anxious every morning to get up and go to work because I'm always anticipating what's next. It just feels good to be working—I think that's the most pleasurable thing—and second is just being right here, seeing things realized, having a hand in it. Standing back and watching something, that's good, and I know most architects live for that, when they see something going up and framed out. But actually making it happen is even better. I don't know if it's quite self-actualization, but it's the closest I've ever come to it.

MATERIALS

Greg: The use of materials has always impressed me, the use of off-the-shelf stuff in an innovative way. And innovative structural approaches—daring, like the Football House. I always enjoy the design of structure. Understanding it is one of the things that I think is the most important in architecture.

Gothic barn rafters in conventional use. *Photo: Michael J. Crosbie.*

Jim: We sometimes push materials to their limits. All of the work has curves in it and it's challenging to figure out, when you've got a form, what material you can use there and make it work. Some materials just won't bend that far. But it's exciting to start building something and not know whether you can really do it. Now we've gotten to the point where we've done enough work to know just how much of a radius different thicknesses of plywood will bend, and we know that you can use a Skil saw to cut a curve as opposed to a slow-moving jigsaw. I think tools have a lot to do with how far you can take something. There are lots of construction tricks that become part of the vocabulary of building.

The design of the early projects was influenced by the Unadilla barn rafters that Steve discovered. They were inexpensive, they had a large selection of different radii, and you could place them on the floor and project them right up in a layered effect. Nobody probably ever used barn rafters other than in the vertical position. Unadilla was very accommodating, in fact they're fans of Jersey Devil because now they're breaking into residential usage. There's a market there that no one ever tapped before.

John: Those uses usually develop out of either some attempt to save money or to surprise. Hopefully both. The trouble is that you don't want to save money and surprise later with something like a leaky roof. We still use materials in ways that they are not normally used, but they tend to be at the decorative level. A flower pot light fixture—Jim's kind of expertise—is a great use for a flower pot and an inexpensive

Unadilla barn rafters in the Snail House. *Photo: Michael J. Crosbie.*

light fixture. That type of response often comes out of, well, "What are we going to use up there?" "Well, let's use some old bottles." Steve knows the Watts Towers, people have seen it, Heineken was trying to make bricks out of bottles. It's not commonly done, but the notion's around of using old materials like that.

Jim: In overcoming the designed use of an object, you have to "design backwards" to use it in a new way. That's the whole notion of the use of materials out of context. People are familiar with the thing in its understood usage and when it's put into a new context they do a flip on it, they react to it, and everybody can identify with it. It's like a jolt: "That shouldn't be there, but it works well." That's the way I think materials should be dealt with. Just because we use asphalt shingles on a roof doesn't mean you can't use them elsewhere. Or Astroturf. I'm always finding places to put it but nobody will go for it, at least not yet.

A great place to generate ideas and see materials out of context is junkyards, especially the ones that stockpile reclaimed materials. During the Hill House project there was a fabulous place in San Mateo. It had everything from bent nails to torpedoes. I really enjoyed going there, rummaging through the piles, looking in bins.

I think folk architecture comes about by a very similar process, because there's a lot of ordinary objects that can be used and can be very beautiful. It could be junk to some people, but if used properly it can enhance and enrich a space.

Terra-cotta flower pot as a light fixture in the Hill House. *Photo: Michael J. Crosbie.*

John: Materials are just that: they're very tactile, very visual, and they smell and even taste. They're the skin and bones of a building, and they should be used with a certain reverence, for where they came from, for what they've done, and for what you are asking them to do.

Steve: It's equally possible, if you have a generous budget, to take a situation where you would expect to see something prefabricated, like a door, and make something really special out of that. The Hill House has a few manholes and flue pipes, but it's got all handmade doors. Every square inch of the thing is crafted. Somewhere along the line I realized, pretty early, that you're not going to compete with tract builders. As things get more and more specialized and standardized, a guy who makes beautiful things with his hands is going to be worth more. I think possibly always.

INSPIRATION

Steve: I think there's a real narrow-minded approach in architecture schools as to what constitutes a building you can learn from. If it isn't Palladio or Lutyens or something from the Italian Renaissance, you don't consider it. I don't want to go on the record as saying Palladio was bad. He was a pretty good architect. But Palladio was a stone mason until he was thirty-five, so he knew what he was doing. His designs were grounded in a sound knowledge of how things were built. I just think there's other, more interesting architecture to look at.

Take vernacular architecture, for example, the traditional buildings in Central Africa, where you have incredibly hostile climatic restraints, severely limited resources, cultural taboos, etc., and people come up with fabulous structures. That's a lesson.

Grain silos. *Photo: Michael J. Crosbie.*

That's architecture. You can learn from industrial buildings and farm buildings as well. A lot of innovative design goes into the materials and structural engineering as well as into daylighting and natural ventilation because these buildings need to be inexpensive. I did my master's thesis on what architects could learn from the mobile home industry. I live in a 1956 Airstream trailer, and the construction technique and the use of space is phenomenal.

John: Buildings influence me, not magazines. I try to stay away from magazines and trends. People are an influence on me also; each of the individuals in Jersey Devil, my friends, my wife Eve, my children, Jonah and Jodi. I have a technical bent from reading a lot of technical literature. Martin Gardner, who until

recently wrote for *Scientific American*, had a column on mathematical games and puzzles, topology, tessellation, geometry, and the like. That always borders on the architectonic.

Steve: At Princeton there was an architecture lab, which was run by Leon Barth. The lab is an enormous shop. Buckminster Fuller used to come there and teach and build domes; Paul Rudolph came with his students

and built things. There's a 24-foot-high glass cube on the back of the lab for building mock-ups. We built the Arthurpod in there. Leon taught us a tremendous amount while we were in school, about tools, about making things, about life.

Greg: In school and throughout your life you admire different architects and things you like to

Steve in front of his 1956 Airstream. *Photo: John Ringel.*

look at. I think the craftsman style of Greene & Greene was a real favorite with me, as was Frank Lloyd Wright.

Jim: I always liked Greene & Greene too, their articulation and detail work. The structure for them was more than just structure, it was the architecture. As a builder I can really appreciate the beauty of what they were doing.

John: If you go to a small town like Stockton, New Jersey, or any number of old towns, there are a lot of places that are decorated. Somebody put a lot of craftsmanship in spaces and items that are not typically, because of cost, decorated nowadays. I think a lot of people have a piece of that in their past, and that's something that we try to draw from in our own work. They grew up in a house that had nothing to do with what modern architecture currently is stating to be the correct style. But it had a banister with a great curve and a beautifully carved ornament on it. Or it had a hunk of stained glass somewhere. And people relate to that. That's "nice stuff," and they grew up with it. There's a piece of architecture that everybody's seen that's not necessarily stylistically correct, but it had some care in it, and craftsmanship, and excitement. The things that Jersey Devil does, in one way or another, break away from the norm, or the ordinary, or the mundane. And people take a second glance; it reminds them, perhaps.

Steve: The method of making things, the way we do it—I'd say Dave Sellers, a design/build architect in Vermont, was the father of that as far as I'm concerned. Dave is a great guy, a fabulous teacher, lecturer, and storyteller. We saw design/build projects in magazines when I was in school—Ant Farm, Prickly

Mountain Project, Haus-Rucker Company in Europe. It wasn't an original move on our part, I could see guys doing it all around. But we may be some of the last. Somewhere along the line the thread's been broken.

POSTERITY

Steve: The Hoagie House is pretty big, about as big as you can get in this kind of residential business. I mean there are bigger homes, but we worry a bit about the social responsibility of building a house this large. These kinds of houses will get built, though. If we didn't build it, surely someone else would, and the architect would probably design it so that it would need its own power plant just to run it. So if big houses are going to get built they might as well get built well and be energy efficient. Take something like the Roto-Lid. It's potentially a really good product to use on commercial and industrial buildings all over the world, and it's being prototyped here.

Greg: I hope people appreciate the fact that we've taken something so big and there's still going to be the same care and attention to detail that we've had in all the other projects, and a refinement in those details. The refinement in thought and detail in all the projects shows a progression.

Steve: Everyone should get better as they get older. Even when you are sixty or seventy there are still going to be some surprises, but you get a better feel for it. That's the thing about architecture—it's not something you learn how to do and then do it. The way the projects connect to each other is not that they're related so much in terms of form. You're obviously smarter, you've learned the lessons of one and you go on to the next.

Decorative newel post with the builders' names at the Silo House. *Photo: Michael J. Crosbie.*

John: Not everyone responds to Jersey Devil's architecture. Some people don't know what they're looking at; it doesn't meet a fixed stereotype. Above and beyond that there are a lot of people who have the kid's reaction: "Hey, that's pretty exciting."

Jim: I think people look at the buildings and get as excited about them as we do. When we step back from a project and try to visualize something or to look at what we've just put up, we chuckle amongst ourselves. "Hey, that's great!" Hopefully other people will respond the same way, it will hit a sympathetic chord. I think people find it humorous, which it should be. It's sort of musical architecture, architecture as sculpture. It elicits a response from people. I think people aren't exposed to much variation from the norm. Then all of a sudden they realize that a house can be something really individualistic, really expressionistic. There are people fashioning really fabulous structures in the backwoods with their hatchets and rudimentary tools. They aren't trained architects, just people out there building dwellings for themselves and not being restricted by any preconceptions of what that building should be. I think architecture is still alive, the individual expression is still there.

John: I think there's a chance that some of our projects will be considered frivolous and extravagant. There's a chance that some of them will be considered inspirational in the way that everybody is inspired by things, not that they'd necessarily do it, but they'll say, "It's just amazing that they did that. It's just amazing." It would be good if they thought that. I guess I'd like them to see that, I'd like them to respond to certain things, to walk in and say that it's a nice place, it's a nice detail. Just a gut reaction.

Steve: I just like to build. I think architecture has to be socially responsible. I think energy efficiency is a way to deal with today's problems, so that we don't have a nuclear future. It's a way of effecting social change in that you have to change a guy's life, the client, give him a few options. I think it's a shame that 95 percent of the housing in this country gets built before the people who are going to live in it even see it.

Unfortunately, the most imaginative people are not going in this direction now. It's rare to find an architecture student who's highly intelligent, really creative and motivated, who likes to build, who sees building as a way to do architecture, or is interested in energy anymore. The talented designers are going into classicism, neorationalism; they're going into the more trendy stuff, and social responsibility is not one of them. Building is not one of them. Originality doesn't seem to be one of them.

What we do is forever out of style, so we might be on the right track.

The gently curved ramp banister at the Silo House. *Photo: Michael J. Crosbie.*

Snail House
1972

It looks like the Jersey Devil's been here." That was the reaction of the locals as the Snail House, the group's first building, took shape on a suburban site in Forked River, New Jersey. The Jersey Devil is a mischievous imp of South Jersey lore who takes great pleasure in scaring the daylights out of people. As John tells the story, the group couldn't pass up this bit of local history and so they assumed the name.

The client for this house was a Princeton University steamfitter named Smitty, who approached Steve and John about building a home for his family near the Jersey shore in the state's Pine Barrens region. The two and a cadre of helpers promptly moved on location and started work.

The unusual shape is due to practical considerations regarding sunlight, ventilation, and privacy. To allow natural light while omitting views in, the curved ribbon windows spiral from east to west, catching the sun as it moves across the southern sky. Natural ventilation through the house is aided by the hollow central core, which acts as a gigantic chimney, drawing cool air from the basement. The shape also reduces the volume of the house by 40 percent (you can enclose more space with less material with a dome form), allowing it to be built on Smitty's slender budget.

The manhole sections are stacked by crane.
Photo: Steve Badanes.

But the Snail House isn't exactly a dome, hence its name. As you walk around the house it appears more like an exploding, overturned grapefruit half, detonated by a stick of dynamite that rises from its center. In plan it resembles the expanding volutes of a snail's shell, which unfold as you move from the south entry, through the living room and dining area, finally culminating in the bedroom and a loft above. In section the house expands as well, faithfully replicating the unfolding of the plan. "John got the idea of putting the tower in the center and just increasing the sections in size," says Steve, "so it becomes a spiral in both plan and section."

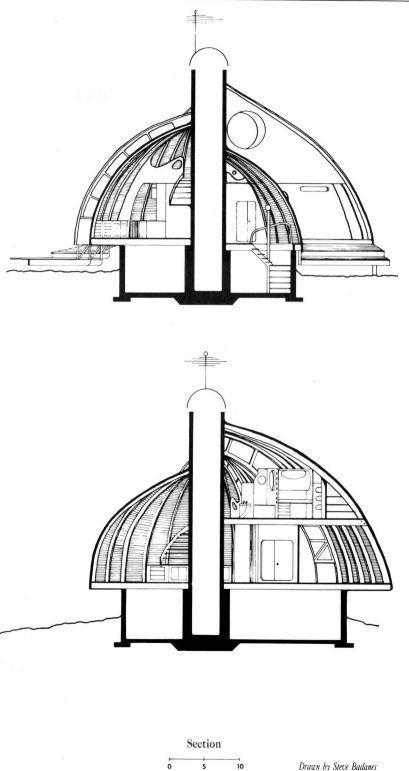

The radial deck is framed. *Photo: Steve Badanes.*

Section

0   5   10

Drawn by Steve Badanes

The novel form was achieved through Jersey Devil's inventive use of some fairly unorthodox building materials. Steve wanted a large thermal mass in the center of the structure. His first impulse was to build a masonry tower out of manhole blocks, which are essentially curved cinder blocks. "A supplier I called said, 'Why don't you use manhole sections and stack them up?' " The sections were 4 feet in diameter, 4 feet high, and weighed 2 tons apiece. Steve ordered eight of them and rented a crane to stack them in place on a heavily reinforced concrete pad set 6 feet below grade. "We stacked four of them and they started leaning way over to the side. The crane driver was laughing," remembers Steve, although it didn't seem very funny at the time. A wooden frame with crosshairs and plumb bobs was rigged up to keep the sections true as each one was stacked, 32,000 pounds in all.

Downview from the tower as the deck is sheathed. *Photo: John Ringel.*

The house fully sheathed. *Photo: Steve Badanes.*

The rafters are tied in. *Photo: Steve Badanes.*

Framed out from this core is a radial deck, supported by a reinforced concrete block foundation. The deck extends beyond the foundation wall to allow natural ventilation through louvers underneath. Next came construction of the curved sections. Steve had known of a company in New York state that manufactured curved barn rafters. "I thought they were fabulous looking, they were cheap, and we could do something really sculptural with them." A few dozen off-the-shelf laminated rafters of varying radii were ordered from the Unadilla Silo Company (which would continue to be a faithful supplier of building materials for future Jersey Devil projects). These were

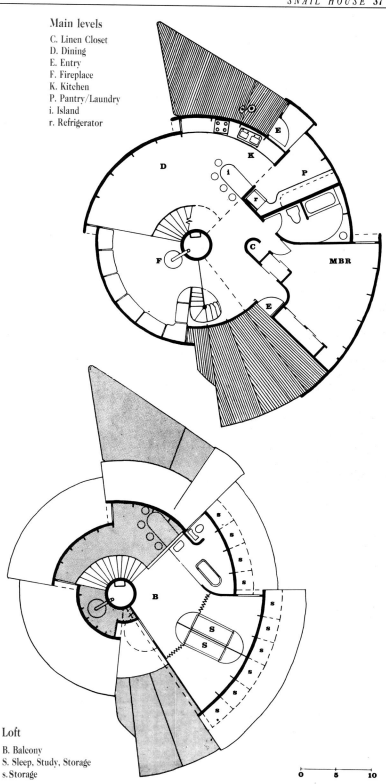

Main levels

C. Linen Closet
D. Dining
E. Entry
F. Fireplace
K. Kitchen
P. Pantry/Laundry
i. Island
r. Refrigerator

View up toward the rafters' apex. *Photo: Steve Badanes.*

Loft

B. Balcony
S. Sleep, Study, Storage
s. Storage

0   5   10

The house from the southwest.
Photo: Steve Badanes.

The house shortly after completion. *Photo: Steve Badanes.*

framed into the core and then sheathed in cedar, which was left as a warm, natural finish on the interior. Slivers of light and cascading wood ribs are the dominant elements inside the house. Its most exciting space is the loft, where you have a commanding view of the shell as it steps up and around the core, terminating its curl in the plastic bubble window. Outside, to provide thermal and weather protection, urethane foam insulation was sprayed on and then sealed with a coat of cement plaster. Entry decks of cedar were a finishing touch.

Today the Snail House is surrounded by other suburban houses of a conventional stripe. But it still pops out from behind the trees, reminding its staid neighbors that the devil lurks among them.

Detail of the house's curving forms under sunlight. *Photos: Michael J. Crosbie.*

Barrel Deck
1973

From time to time, between large-scale design/build jobs, Jersey Devil has produced some small-scale wonders, one of the earliest of which is this backyard deck for a house in suburban Somerset, New Jersey. The budget for the deck was arrived at via an even swap between the architects and their lawyer client. John and Steve would provide the design and craftsmanship in exchange for materials and the lawyer's services so that John could get a divorce. Fair enough.

Jersey Devil prepared for the deck job as the Snail House neared completion. The materials were bought from a local lumber mill near Forked River—the mill's year supply of 2 × 3 cedar. The program was fairly simple: the client wanted a deck that offered privacy from neighboring yards on either side while providing views toward the back of his property. These requirements generated the boatlike form with high side arms fore and aft that bend gracefully back, which John likens to a Viking ship.

A heated exchange between the two devils began when it

John puts on the finishing touches.
Photo: Steve Badanes.

came time to decide where to place the seating, tables, and other accoutrements. As the two continued to build and shout, John remembers, a helper did all he could to keep him and Steve from braining each other with their hammers. (Impassioned debate and threats of bodily harm are a part of the collective creative process that most design partners politely omit when discussing their work.) "It was really spirited," says John, "arguing madly with each other about which side of the deck we were going to put the plant hanger and whatnot."

When the dust finally settled, the Barrel Deck was complete with two benches and a table between them on one side, with a bench and workspace suitable for a hibachi on the other. The seats and table seem to grow naturally from the floor of the deck as they curl up and around like a roll-top desk out on a picnic. On one end a wooden dowel runs the width of the deck, providing a sunny exposure for hanging plants. It all seems to have been worth the fight, and John has since happily remarried.

Stone House Renovation
1974

Either a former smoke house or ice house, this quaint but unusable 125-year-old stone building was converted by Jersey Devil into a backyard retreat for a plastic surgeon and his wife. The little structure sits poolside to the rear of the main house in a Princeton, New Jersey, neighborhood. It was essentially an empty shell (what John remembers as a "startling void") with a dirt floor depressed 4 feet below the threshold. Fourteen feet above, where the gable roof met the top of the stone walls, a series of tie-beams held the structure together in tension. The clients wanted a two-level study that could double as a guest house. Given these criteria, the problem was to provide a second floor with sufficient headroom while maintaining the rafter bracing. Steve and John combined the two elements—tie-beam and floor—in an ingenious tensile structure that appears to float in mid air: "a handcrafted, wood sculptural item suspended in a

The Stone House, exterior. *Photo: Steve Badanes.*

The warm wood glow of the lower level.
Photo: Steve Badanes.

neutral, sheetrocked, Monopoly board house-shaped volume," as Steve describes it.

The form of this hanging cradle was cribbed from the Barrel Deck. It was prefabricated outside the Stone House with its sloping side members pinned at their joints so that the frame could be folded up, hauled inside, unfolded, and fastened into place. The end of each arm was connected to a rafter and then the pinned joints were nailed in their open position so that the whole structure was rigid. A bridge that extends out from the loft connects to a hand-crafted staircase of fir (with a laminated plywood rail) that sweeps down past the front door, pauses for a landing, and then continues down to the lower level. What was the building inspector's reaction to all this ingenuity? "He poked his head through the door," says John, "took one look up and then jumped right back out again." He insisted on more bolts and nails, which were installed.

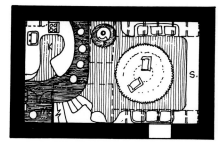

Lower Levels

F. Fireplace
M. Hot Water Heater, Elec. Box (Landing Above)
S. Bookshelves, Records, etc.
K. Kitchen, Bar

The handbuilt kitchen with salvaged stools.
Photo: Steve Badanes.

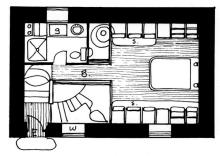

Upper Level

E. Entry
B. Bridge
g. Glass Top (Window/Skylight Below)
s. Seating
w. Window Service to Pool Area

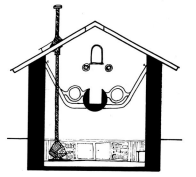

Sections

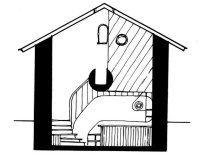

Drawn by Steve Badanes

The loft and bridge are clad in fir flooring and the railings at the end of the loft take the shape of a pair of spectacles. When viewed in section, the railings, bridge, and loft arms look like a big rubber nose and glasses—a not-so-subtle reference to the cosmetic qualities of the client's craft. Next to the bridge is a bathroom whose red flocked rubber ball doorstops are a good example of everyday objects fulfilling architectural functions in a new context.

The upper level has lots of sunlight, brought in by skylights between each rafter directly over the loft arms. This also enhances the illusion of the structure being pinned to thin air. The end walls have arched windows with frames and sash entirely site-built. The window above the bed even has a built-in folding ladder for safe exit in case of fire. In contrast, the lower level is dark and cozy. Here the doctor has a study with a free-standing metal fireplace and a kitchen complete with custom-built serving counter and stools that Steve salvaged from a

Detail of bridge, rail, and hanging loft. *Photo: Steve Badanes.*

demolished diner. The kitchen receives natural light from a splayed window well that is intersected by the upper level. The plexiglass in the south windows facing the pool is curved, which not only makes it more rigid but lends an organic quality, as though the house is actually breathing.

All things considered, this is a great internal transplant for an old building. Its playhouse scale, plus all the fun and games inside, would make anyone feel like a kid again.

The steps down from the entrance with places to hide. *Photo: Steve Badanes.*

Overview of the loft. *Photo: Steve Badanes.*

Detail of laminated plywood rail. *Photo: Steve Badanes.*

Helmet House
1974

From a distance, through the trees, the Helmet House could be mistaken for something ditched by an extraterrestrial with engine trouble or the shell of a prehistoric tortoise that waddled up from the nearby lake. It's actually a remote retreat for a modern-day caveman that won for Jersey Devil *National Enquirer*'s "Weird Home Award."

When the architects arrived on the site in southern New Hampshire, they found a clearing in the woods by a lake, with a 35-foot-high outcropping of granite. Steve describes the client for the Helmet House as a "kind of Don Quixote type of guy who wanted his guests to feel somewhat ill at ease." The idea was to make the rock outcropping the interior of the house without partitions of any kind, protected from the elements by a large roof. The quest then focused on how to make the roof.

Sheathing the rafters. *Photo: Steve Badanes.*

Steve and John returned to their Unadilla Silo Company catalogue for a series of pointed, laminated barn rafters. The end result was a design with a Gothic, medieval quality—a small nod to the revival style of many of the region's farm structures. John built a study model (which subsequently got stepped on) showing how the rafters would spill down from the top of the outcropping, tipping over the rockface, as Steve says, "like a gigantic Slinky," with the structure exposed inside.

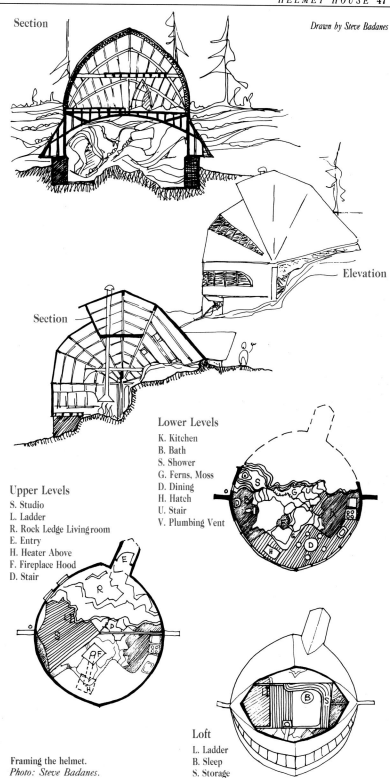

Section

Drawn by Steve Badanes

Elevation

Section

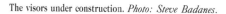
The visors under construction. *Photo: Steve Badanes.*

Framing the helmet.
Photo: Steve Badanes.

Upper Levels

S. Studio
L. Ladder
R. Rock Ledge Living room
E. Entry
H. Heater Above
F. Fireplace Hood
D. Stair

Lower Levels

K. Kitchen
B. Bath
S. Shower
G. Ferns, Moss
D. Dining
H. Hatch
U. Stair
V. Plumbing Vent

Loft

L. Ladder
B. Sleep
S. Storage

The first stage was construction of the bottom-most curved vertical wall, which was wood-frame box beam construction jutting out like the prow of a ship, supported by a concrete block foundation. As each pair of barn rafters was fastened together, it was tipped up and braced into place. For sheathing the rafters, Jersey Devil chose a combination of inexpensive building materials: prepainted Homasote sheathing was applied and covered with a layer of closed cell styrofoam board stock. This was then plastered with ferrocement over chicken wire.

The main entrance into the Helmet House is through a door at the top of the outcropping, framed in a miniature Gothic arch. The interior then tumbles before you, down a few rocks to the upper living room, a few more steps down to the wooden platform that serves as a studio, and then a boulder "stairway" down to the kitchen, living, and dining area. Light is admitted by three strips of "visors" that extend over the helmet, exposing the framing inside. The shower and toilet are barely tucked away behind the shelf of a rock, offering, as Steve points out, some visual privacy but not a great deal of olfactory or acoustical privacy. High above your head is a loft for sleeping and down below there is an open pit for heating and cooking. Given these surroundings, protected by a helmet of weird repute, everyone should feel properly ill at ease.

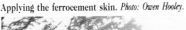

Applying the ferrocement skin. Photo: Owen Hooley.

Rock grotto shower. *Photo: Steve Badanes.*

The house amid the trees. *Photo: Steve Badanes.*

Silo House
1975

The Silo House in Lambertville, New Jersey, marks a transition for Jersey Devil. It shows refinements that, due to budget restraints, were lacking in some earlier projects. The most striking of these is the detailing and the house's welcoming, human scale. This was also the first Jersey Devil project for Jim, who was finally coaxed down from his yurt in Vermont by Steve's postcards. His presence is seen in the house's handcrafted quality.

The Silo House was built for Charlie and Mary Lou Swift, who had returned to the states after eight years in Tanzania. With their children grown, the Swifts wanted a small, efficient house that was close to nature. As Steve worked on the design with Charlie and Mary Lou, one element continually cropped up: circles. No matter what he came back with, the Swifts pushed for spaces in the round, which reminded them of the conical roofed huts they had grown to appreciate in Africa. Working

The house's north elevation. *Photo: Steve Badanes.*

with circles, Steve came up with a plan of startling clarity and simplicity: three separate zoned areas for sleeping, living, and working, each separated by airlock entries and joined by a circulation spine. The ultimate bubble diagram.

Jersey Devil turned again to the Unadilla Silo Company for the building components. An order for six 8-foot-high prefabricated grain silos "got a bunch of raised eyebrows from the company," says John. "They suggested that we could just as easily order one 48 footer." The six spruce silos arrived in kit form and were assembled, each pod having an inner and outer silo with urethane foam insulation in between.

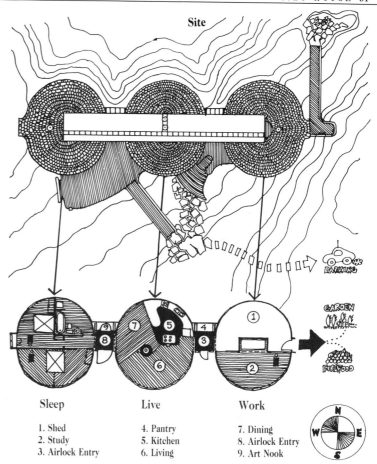

Site

Sleep
1. Shed
2. Study
3. Airlock Entry

Live
4. Pantry
5. Kitchen
6. Living

Work
7. Dining
8. Airlock Entry
9. Art Nook

Drawn by Steve Badanes

Interior under construction. *Photo: Steve Badanes.*

Framing for silo skins. *Photo: Steve Badanes.*

Jim remembers the whole construction process as lively, with the Swifts helping out every day. Meanwhile, Steve had his hands full keeping up with the large crew working on the job. "He always promotes people to be creative on their own," says Jim, "but at times it was totally out of control." At one point a couple of woodworkers began to cut a row of bunny rabbits into the door trim. Steve thought it was great until Charlie came by and expressed some doubts. The bunnies lost.

The idea to add active solar space heating came up during construction. The state of technology was fairly crude at this point, but Jersey Devil's hot air system shows an inventive use of materials. The site-built collector is made of used aluminum printer's plates painted black. The front is glazed with two layers of Kalwall .025-inch Sunlite Premium fiberglass sheets. The airspace behind this panel is filled with galvanized expanded metal plastering lath. The entire assembly is finished in a highly absorbent black paint, the same coating used on the inside of cameras. Besides direct gain from the sun's rays, additional light reflects off the aluminum visors above and below the collector. The collector and its components are protected by a curved roof housing that is sheathed with white hardtop automobile vinyl. A 15-ton rockbed beneath the center silo stores the heated air,

Secondary entrance to work silo. *Photo: Steve Badanes.*

The secondary entrance with its bowed side lights. *Photo: Steve Badanes.*

which is then pumped into the house through a plenum. Wood stoves supply backup heating and each silo can be closed off with sliding doors. The site-built truss that supports the collector above the silos is glazed, bringing natural light in from overhead. Directly above each entrance is a circular void that catches prevailing breezes, inducing summer ventilation through round pivot windows.

Between the sleeping and living silos is the main entry, defined by a wide, yellow door.

Sections

The Swifts in their sunlit living area. *Photo: John Senzer.*

The little vestibule inside has a handmade cabinet and niche for displaying the Swifts' collection of African art objects. Each silo has exposed rafters articulating the conical drywall ceiling. All cabinets (as well as the toilet seat) are handbuilt, and a huge antique cook stove dominates the kitchen/dining area. The flooring is made of fir "roofers," which were commonly used before the advent of plywood. "The Swifts'

rustic esthetic allowed us to use the roofers for flooring," says John, "which was a cost saving." Other material shortcuts include doors that were salvaged from a nearby school and door handles that are mahogany cement floats.

Outside, free-form decks flow around the silos, accessible by steps or a lenticular truss ramp

that leads you to the front door. According to Steve, "The decks relate to special parts of the site, like significant trees or moss-covered boulders." A ramp on the east side that curls up to the workshop is used for wheeling in firewood. In 1979, John built a rustic carport and in 1980, a firewood shelter out back. Steve and Greg added a garden room to the east entry in 1982.

The Silo House has withstood the test of time. Although its solar collector is antique by today's standards (and may one day find a place in the Smithsonian), the house has grown better with age, much like the woods surrounding it.

Sunlight is admitted during winter. *Photo: Steve Badanes.*

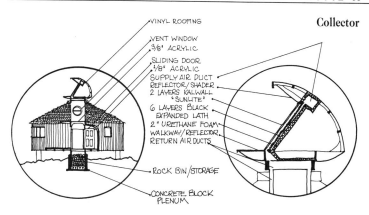

Collector

VINYL ROOFING
VENT WINDOW
3/8" ACRYLIC
SLIDING DOOR
1/8" ACRYLIC
SUPPLY AIR DUCT
REFLECTOR/SHADER
2 LAYERS KALWALL "SUNLITE"
6 LAYERS BLACK EXPANDED LATH
2" URETHANE FOAM
WALKWAY/REFLECTOR
RETURN AIR DUCTS
ROCK BIN/STORAGE
CONCRETE BLOCK PLENUM

The front entry from the southwest. *Photo: John Senzer.*

Football House
1976

A quarter mile from the San Andreas Fault, in the mountainous, northern California countryside, the Football House sits poised above a 45-degree sloping site, appearing to defy gravity. The house, actually an addition to an existing residence, was built by Steve and Jim for a friend who wanted a place that could be used as a study or guest quarters.

Directly beside the existing house is a beautiful stand of redwoods. Rather than disturb these giants, a truss bridge was used to connect the old with the new. The addition achieves its structural gymnastics through the use of two lenticular trusses that act as bearing walls. The tremendous slope was one of the reasons why these trusses, each of which could be supported at a single point, were chosen. "We realized that we had to minimize the

foundation work," says Jim, "because we couldn't get any earth moving equipment down there, and anything we designed would have to be dug by hand." Two piers, each 4-feet × 1-foot × 10-feet deep, are anchored into the ground and tied together with a concrete key down slope and below grade. Bolted into

Framing on the house begins precariously. *Photo: Steve Badanes.*

Deck framing nearing completion.
Photo: Jim Adamson.

these piers are tall, vertical frames of fir 2 × 10s that extend the full height of the structure and end in a pyramidal skylight.

The lenticular trusses are integrated into the sidewall framing with decks spanning between. The trusses also allow the building to be completely open to the south, providing solar gain and a breathtaking view. The redwoods must have provided some inspiration too. Steve likens the house to a tree, firmly rooted in the ground and cantilevering out as it grows. As the structure was sheathed in plywood and redwood siding, cutouts were left to articulate the trusses beneath and

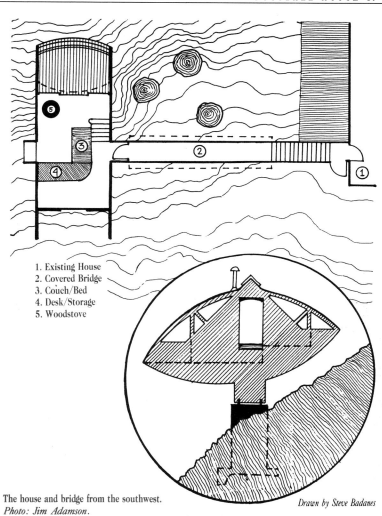

1. Existing House
2. Covered Bridge
3. Couch/Bed
4. Desk/Storage
5. Woodstove

Drawn by Steve Badanes

Detail of bridge framing. *Photo: Jim Adamson.*

The house and bridge from the southwest.
Photo: Jim Adamson.

provide additional views east and west. The curved roof is covered with asphalt shingles, a small restriction the client imposed to relate the addition to the older structure. "The ideal material would have been Astroturf," says Jim. Aside from its structural articulation, Steve says that the football shape has a contingent function. "If a quake comes and the house leaves its moorings, it'll simply roll down the hill, end over end." The architects' suggestion of a goal post at the bottom of the hill didn't reassure the client that he wouldn't end up on the receiving end of a structural fumble.

The house's interior, which was finished by the client, is voluminous—more spacious than you'd expect in a relatively small structure. As you arrive on the upper level and look up, your eyes trace the surface of the vault as it describes a gentle curve, not unlike that of a football after the kickoff. The redwood trim is slender and crisp, and all workspaces, cabinets, and bookshelves are built in. A wood stove sits on the lower level, providing backup heating. Outside the south wall's sliding glass doors is a redwood deck, which appears to fold down like a drawbridge—the culmination of spectacular views, sunlight, and some major league structural design.

Detail of rail on the outside deck. *Photo: Steve Badanes.*

The house balances on its scant foundation.
Photo: Steve Badanes.

The house and its deck. *Photo: Jim Adamson.*

The house from the northeast.
Photo: Steve Badanes.

Running Bureaus
1976

Traveling south from the Bay Area to Los Angeles between jobs, Steve and Pat Patterson, a friend and artist, picked up some work along the way at a boarding school in Los Olivos. "We stopped there just to visit a friend of mine who was the headmaster," says Steve. "He said that if we wanted to, we could stay and do some work for the school." The two dubbed themselves "Micro Maintenance Service," bought some uniforms, and took over the school shop to build thirty bureaus.

The bureaus are made of pine plywood, sanded and finished with a sprayed urethane lacquer. Carved drawer pulls (both right-handed and left-handed models) were used instead of hardware to reduce cost and maintenance. Components for all thirty were cut before a prototype was assembled, which was a wrong move. "They were all sort of wobbly," Steve confesses, so 2 × 4s were used in back for bracing and decoration.

Why "Running Bureaus"? Steve says that when the bureaus were complete, Pat suggested lining them up for a group photo. "And that was the same week that Christo was doing his 'Running Fence' near San Francisco, so a sympathetic gesture seemed appropriate."

Steve shows his handiwork. *Photo: Pat Patterson.*

Pat and the Running Bureaus. *Photo: Steve Badanes.*

Hill House
1977-1979

A few years ago when George and Adele Norton bought their hilltop site in the Santa Cruz Mountains, they knew some day that they would build a house there. It really is a perfect spot, 2,300 feet above the Pacific with views of the ocean, the city of San Francisco, and the bay, 50 miles to the northwest. "This is a special site," says George, "and it required a special house."

There's no doubt that the Nortons got what they bargained for when they asked Steve and Jim to ply their craft. Along with the Nortons, the local planning body agreed that the site's uniqueness called for a house that was unobtrusive, one that blended into the setting and enhanced the environment. A simple solution presented itself: make the hill the house.

Construction started by carving a shelf in the hilltop, into which the house would nestle. Concrete footings, north bearing wall, slab, Trombe wall, even a headboard in what would be the bedroom were poured, 175 cubic yards in all. Culvert sections were inserted into the forms to create portholes, a recurring theme throughout the house. The south wall curves, following the contour, and supports columns 4 feet on center that in turn support a curved box beam that carries the

Aerial view of the house. *Photo: Bob Moore.*

roof. Stock lenticular trusses were ordered from the Trus Joist Company and placed in a fan fashion spanning 24 feet, creating an interior devoid of bearing walls. Pine decking covered the trusses, a plywood diaphragm came next, rigid foam insulation, then a hot mopped roof, crushed stone for drainage, base rock, and finally topsoil. Thus the roof completed the hilltop once again.

Section

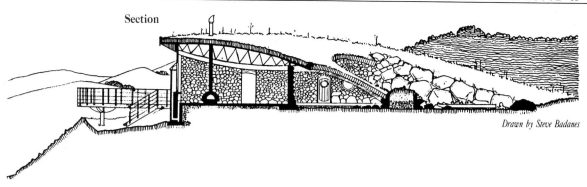

Drawn by Steve Badanes

Concrete forms under construction. *Photo: Steve Badanes.*

Poured concrete complete with Bay Area to the north. *Photo: Steve Badanes.*

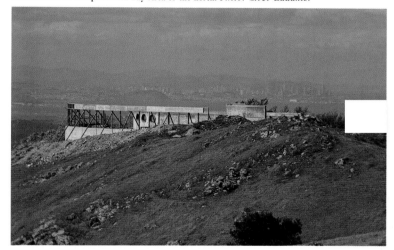

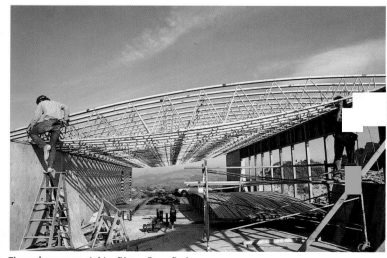

The roof trusses are tied in. *Photo: Steve Badanes.*

Because the interior walls were to be nonbearing, it was possible to make them curved, straight, bowed, undulating–whatever the situation seemed to suggest. Some are covered with stone veneer, others with stucco over wire lath. All stop a foot below the ceiling, getting the point across that they aren't supporting anything except themselves. This allows an uninterrupted view across the ceiling surface, which changes from stucco, to open truss, to laminated fir. Plexiglass glazing between the wall and the ceiling stops noise transmission.

One enters the house via a courtyard in the round, alive with Adele's collection of native Californian plants. Winds on the mountaintop sometimes reach 100 miles an hour (during construction the hot tub took flight and landed in a tree) but the house's contour allows these winds to blow right over, barely rustling the plants. The roof, covered with grass, dips down into the courtyard as a snout supplying water for a "huge flowerpot." You can imagine this appendage as a tendon, keeping the house firmly anchored to the hilltop.

Spatially, the layout is reasonably conventional, with separate wings for children and adults separated by shared living space, what Steve calls a "curved rancher." The living room, dining room, and kitchen bend around behind the bank of windows.

Roof trusses completely installed. *Photo: Steve Badanes.*

One of Curtis Schreier's handmade doors. *Photo: Steve Badanes.*

South wall with its curving roof framing. *Photo: Steve Badanes.*

The dining area. Table by John Kapel. Painting by Michael Moore. *Photo: Steve Badanes.*

Detail of Curtis Schreier's handmade door hardware. *Photo: Jim Adamson.*

The kitchen area. *Photo: Steve Badanes.*

Overview of living room and kitchen area.
Photo: Steve Badanes.

Down the hall to the east are two bedrooms, two bathrooms, a family room, a wine cellar, and the garage. To the west is an office, master bedroom, and a fern-sprouting bath. The inside finishes are hardly conventional, though. Artisans and craftsmen stopping by to visit lent their skills. All the woodwork is hand-made, from the doors to the kitchen counter and cabinets.

The attention to handcrafted detail gives this house an absorbing scale, a character that makes you want to touch everything. And the details are graspable, just right for the fingertips.

Jim devised a number of site-designed and -built light fixtures that make you look at least twice: ducts droop from walls to throw light instead of air, over-turned flowerpots amid the trusses cast a warm glow to the tile floor below, and gooseneck

lamps slither out from the culverts and back-lit Nerf balls. Other materials are put to unintended uses, such as Almaden bottles as clerestories, Perrier bottles as glazing in the garage wall culverts, and terra-cotta flue pipes that hold the wine room's cache.

View from the living area to dining area along south wall. *Photo: Steve Badanes.*

Master bedroom with its curved ceiling and cast-in-place headboard. *Photo: Steve Badanes.*

The house is energy efficient as well. Being earthsheltered, it has the benefits of protection from wind, fire, and thermal extremes. The foot-thick Trombe wall directly below the curved window wall sends warm air into the house by natural convection during the cool months. In summer, the warm air is vented out, drawing cool air inside. Well water is pumped by a windmill into an 8,000-gallon tank and is then gravity-fed to the house. Solar collectors near the garage supply hot water.

It seems as though the Hill House has been well received by its natural surroundings. George occasionally finds goats grazing on the roof. And from high above, the house appears to be little more than the hilltop's satisfied grin.

The entry door and stone veneer entry wall from the courtyard. *Photo: Steve Badanes.*

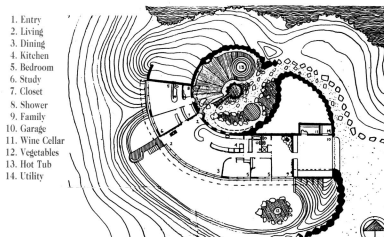

1. Entry
2. Living
3. Dining
4. Kitchen
5. Bedroom
6. Study
7. Closet
8. Shower
9. Family
10. Garage
11. Wine Cellar
12. Vegetables
13. Hot Tub
14. Utility

The courtyard from the roof. *Photo: Steve Badanes.*

Viewing deck off the living area. © Peter
Aaron ESTO.

The house in the setting sun. *Photo: Steve Badanes.*

Aerial view of the house.
Photo: Bob Moore.

Airplane House
1980

Southeast Colorado has a surreal landscape. Huge land masses pop up from nowhere for no apparent reason, cloud formations and electrical storms race up and down the foothills, and the clear night sky frequently displays meteor showers and proximate planets. The locals here spot UFOs for sport and a few have had some pretty close encounters. So when a retired couple—both avid private pilots—sought out Steve and Jim to design and build a house, Jersey Devil was sure to feel at home responding to this bizarre geographic and cultural context. The house is sited in a huge subdivision yet to be built, at the end of a cul-de-sac visible only from the air. It was Steve's hope that since this was the first house in the neighborhood, future residents would respond to the existing architecture.

Acknowledging the most potent force in the region—the climate—the structure is axially oriented north/south, with living spaces concentrated on the south side, storage and utility spaces on the north. The house is wood frame construction, heavily insulated, and covered from top to bottom with corrugated asphalt panels. The roof panels are

The west elevation amid snow storm.
Photo: Steve Badanes.

painted silver to reflect the heat of the high summer sun, while the walls are dark brown to absorb warmth in the winter. The south wall is a composition of various size windows and clerestories that admit winter sunlight, which is absorbed into the red-tinted concrete floor and low partitions that are actually steel tanks holding 1,200 gallons of water. The Sunflake windows with sliding insulated pocket panels reduce heat gain in the summer and provide night insulation in the winter. Also on the south wall is a site-built solar collector for preheating domestic hot water. Thermal barriers around the house include earth berming to the northeast and northwest, airspace in the roof, and an airlock entry.

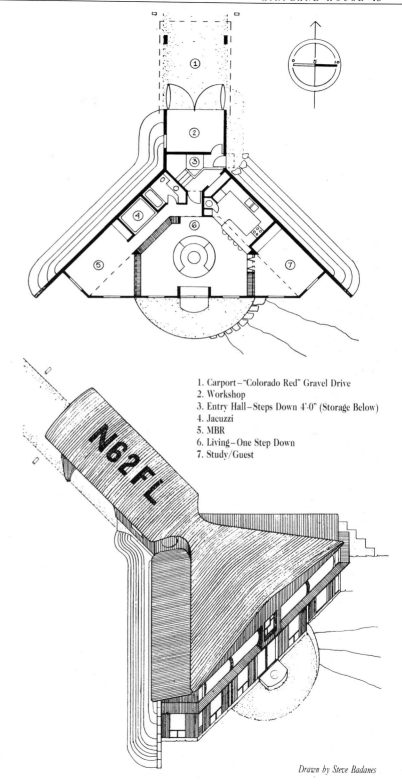

Framed structure from the north.
Photo: Steve Badanes.

Framing nearly complete.
Photo: Steve Badanes.

1. Carport—"Colorado Red" Gravel Drive
2. Workshop
3. Entry Hall—Steps Down 4'-0" (Storage Below)
4. Jacuzzi
5. MBR
6. Living—One Step Down
7. Study/Guest

Drawn by Steve Badanes

Approaching it from the winding, unpaved road, the house emerges from the desert terrain like a scaly, beady-eyed rattler showing its fangs. There is plenty of precedent, for the surrounding countryside is crawling with reptiles. But it's quite harmless—no

The southeast corner. *Photo: Steve Badanes.*

Approach to the house with eastern sun. *Photo: Steve Badanes.*

more than a stuffed snake to dissuade strangers from disturbing the privacy-loving residents.

Walking around the house from either side, the structure unfolds like a bird in flight, although its silvery roof and tight angles make it more aeronautic than avian. The south wall's soffit bends and twists, defining a warped surface between the roofline and the building wall—another aerodynamic contour. The entry is found on the east side (just around the corner from the carport), guarded by a space frame tower topped with a T.V. antenna. The tight foyer space,

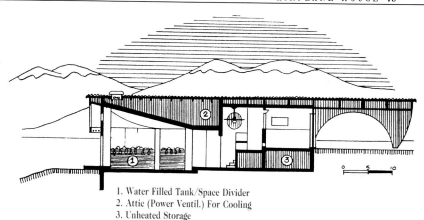

1. Water Filled Tank/Space Divider
2. Attic (Power Ventil.) For Cooling
3. Unheated Storage

The interior shortly after completion. *Photo: Steve Badanes.*

The carport shows its fangs. *Photo: Steve Badanes.*

lit from above through translucent fiberglass portholes, works to contrast the large volume you are about to enter. The plan fans out, distributing, from west to east, the master bedroom with bath and open spa area, the spacious living and dining area, a kitchen tucked just behind it, and an office/guest area. The spaces are defined by wall panels with cutouts that fan across the plan as if tracking the sun. The spaces most east and west have low ceilings, while the living/dining area ceiling soars toward the high windows on the south wall. The ceiling surfaces warp along the roof ridge to bounce light around. The whole interior appears to mimic flight—low wings on either side provide lift for the center fuselage climbing in altitude.

Hoping to use some indigenous materials as decorative motifs, Steve, Jim, and Donna took a trip to the only industry in town, the Do-Ray Lamp Company, maker of those colored lights you see on tractor trailers and police cars. "We took a tour of the factory," Jim says, "and then walked through the warehouse picking out stuff we thought we could use." Not far from the building site was a pile of white plastic 8-inch drainage pipe left over from installation of the water and sewer lines. This was cut into small sections, drilled out, and fitted with the

The southwest view, shortly after completion. *Photo: Steve Badanes.*

lamps. One fixture was installed over the front door, while two bubble lamps found a place over the carport. Not only decorative, they're also very handy in shedding some light on this twilight zone.

Recent photo of entry with landscaping completed. *Photo: Steve Badanes.*

L.A. Deck
1981

High above Hollywood in L.A.'s Silver Lake district, this deck makes the most of its hilltop locale, with plenty of space for sunning, bathing, and viewing. The client, a friend of Jim's, wanted an addition to replace a small greenhouse, and a deck that would cover most of his backyard, which he didn't relish taking care of. In a reversal of their usual roles, Jim came up with the design concept, dealt with the local bureaucracy, and hustled materials, while Steve worked with Donna on a 9-to-5 construction job. "Steve had a great time articulating the design," says Jim, "not having to worry about the headaches of getting on the phone and lining things up, which I don't like doing."

The small backyard, covered with jade plants, sloped steeply to the street below, offering the opportunity to cantilever the deck out over the hill. Jim removed the old greenhouse structure and saved the pieces to glaze the now enlarged dining room. This space shares the deck's spectacular view and is tiled with terra cotta, giving it a warm glow. The warped soffit

The hot tub with V-shaped bench at left. *Photo: Jim Adamson.*

and heavy-looking fascia above the dining room conceals a small bedroom deck above. The floating overhang also shades the dining room.

The deck itself responds to the California architectural tradition of finely detailed organic woodworking (in the manner of Greene & Greene, and Maybeck). Jim canted the deck's oval-shaped main part out from the house at 45 degrees, orienting it towards the view. On one side is a mahogany hot tub, around which the cedar deck steps up and then gently slopes back down, becoming a seat. On the other side of the oval the deck curves around again, this time lined with seats that end in a curl. Perpendicular to this large oval is a smaller one that sprouts a light tower and flower pot.

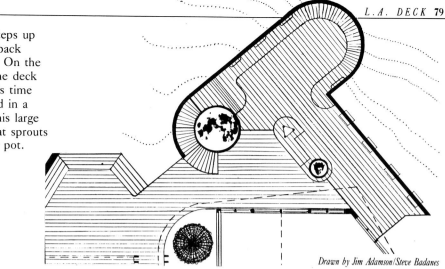

Drawn by Jim Adamson/Steve Badanes

Overview of main and bedroom decks. *Photo: Steve Badanes.*

Other materials include terra-cotta flue pipes, reiterating the oval geometry, which puncture the long, straight deck railing; terra-cotta flower pots used as light fixtures; and cream-colored stucco facing for the deck and dining room. Together, the tile, stucco, and curves constitute what Steve describes as "Taco-Stand Modern."

The light tower that dominates the deck at its center was site-built by Jim and given to the client as a "deck-warming" gift. This mechanical, vertical element, which plays off the deck's organic, horizontal character, was assembled from bits and pieces that Jim collected. The lower tower was bought in a radio supply store. This is topped by three glass light globes from a local junk shop. Next, three funnels and galvanized pipe of

diminishing size climb into the clouds, reflecting the light below. Finally, the tower is crowned with a toilet tank float finial, its stem thrust triumphantly over the flush of Tinsel Town.

View of the deck from dining room. *Photo: Jim Adamson.*

Overview of main deck from bedroom deck.
Photo: Jim Adamson.

The deck hovers over the tinsel glow of Hollywood. *Photo: Jim Adamson.*

Lake of the Woods Deck
1982

Another break between large-scale building projects allowed time for another deck, this one bigger than any other to date. Steve and Donna returned east to settle in Locust Grove, Virginia, for a few months so both could work on this sundeck for a friend's vacation home.

The existing deck had made it to an advanced stage of rot without completely falling off the side of the house, but beyond structural instability it had an identity problem. "It had sort of a Tyrolian fascia," says Steve, which didn't seem to relate to anything in particular. The new deck needed to provide plenty of space for sunning (a tricky problem because it would be located on the house's

Deck from the southeast corner. *Photo: Steve Badanes.*

View of the deck from the house's north side.
Photo: Steve Badanes.

north side), privacy from the neighbors, and a vantage point for spectacular views over the lake.

To take care of the rotting problem, pressure-treated yellow pine was used for the framing. The decking itself is cedar. Steve brought the deck out as far north as possible, beyond the shadow of the house and into the sunlight. He pulled it out in successive stages, though, in a sawtooth pattern, to give the spaces some variety and to also allude to the lake's wave motion. The high-back seats, which are regenerations of the Barrel Deck, serve the same purpose here: to discourage prying eyes. The far seat, tucked just beneath a tree limb, offers some seclusion. The next has a table for picnicking, cards, or whatever, while the third has a low bench for foot propping. These elements appear to grow right out of the deck like wooden mushrooms.

The tower that rises 16 feet toward the lake was actually built before it was connected to the deck. "It was obvious that if you could get up to that point you'd have a great view," explains Steve, so the tower's elevation was determined by the peek through the trees. It has high-back seats as well that face each other; a veritable high altar for sun worship.

View of the deck and its seats from the east. *Photo: Steve Badanes.*

Deck covered on the east side of the house. *Photo: Steve Badanes.*

The observation tower with lake view. *Photo: Steve Badanes.*

Hot Tub House
1982

Like many rural communities in New Jersey, Stockton is full of old houses dating from the eighteenth and nineteenth centuries. Most have undergone gradual transformations—a room added here, a dormer there—reflecting changes in lifestyle over time and the amazing adaptability of these simple structures. John and Greg have left their own mark on one of these houses—an addition/renovation that successfully combines traditional and contemporary images of home life.

The original house was built in the early 1800s, "a little old house with a stairway in the center and chimneys at both ends," as John describes it. By 1910 the front porch had been added and the basic house shape was a **T**. Forty years later a "modern" kitchen was moved under a shed roof to the rear, followed by a shed-roofed timber frame shell on the house's east side added in the 1960s by the present owner. He wanted an overhaul of these added pieces (save for the porch) with a new kitchen, two bathrooms, a sleeping area, and a hot tub.

Starting around back, the kitchen was completely gutted

Exterior of house with addition on right, topped by solar hot water collector. *Photo: Michael J. Crosbie.*

and reconstructed on a reinforced concrete slab, adding a real foundation for the first time. The basic shed form was maintained but raised to insulate the north wall of the house's older sections. Within this shell the new kitchen extends the full height of the shed, creating a soaring space that seems much larger than it actually is. The center workspace is illuminated by four red warehouse light fixtures. Recessed periphery lighting occurs over the handbuilt counters and cabinets.

Although the white tile floor is real, the walls are actually papered with a white tile/red grout pattern. A new bathroom is located next to the kitchen, screened by a pocket door. A wood stove vented at the ceiling sits beside the entry to the old house from the kitchen, as if portending the more traditional esthetic that lies beyond.

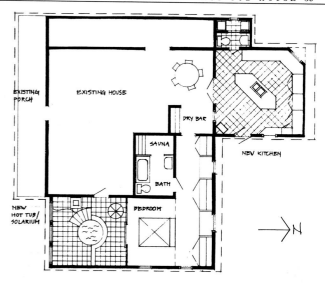

Detail of rail on the balcony level. *Photo: Michael J. Crosbie.*

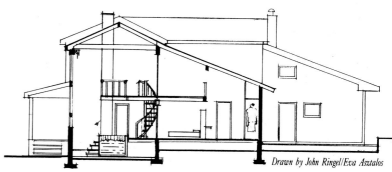

Drawn by John Ringel/Eva Asztalos

Kitchen with center work counter. *Photo: Greg Torchio.*

To get to the 1960s addition from the kitchen, John extended a shed roof to create a passage between the two. A mahogany cabinet with built-in lighting to illuminate art work is located in front of a short staircase up into the wide, welcoming hallway. Birch closets and storage spaces line the hallway's north wall, acting as a thermal barrier. Included is a window seat with folding, solid shutters that can be closed during the winter. A master bathroom is located on the south side. On the east wall are two stained glass windows salvaged by the client years before.

The original addition was little more than a timber frame with a loft. Its southern orientation

Welcoming hallway from original house to bedroom. *Photo: Michael J. Crosbie.*

Timber frame in hallway with bathroom door to right. *Photo: Michael J. Crosbie.*

prompted John to create a window wall for direct-gain solar heating. In front of the windows, down a few steps to maintain privacy, is the redwood hot tub surrounded by a tile floor and redwood shelf/seat. Tucked just around the corner is a shower. The brick chimney and green-painted concrete wall act as a thermal mass to absorb the sun's warmth in the winter. In the summer a solar curtain can be drawn over the window wall. John describes the hot tub room as a solar collector you can live in.

In and around the beefed-up timber frame are pockets of space for sleeping and relaxing, an amazing variety in such a small enclosure. The loft, accessible by a steel circular stair, has a balcony with a handbuilt cherry rail that traces the curve of the hot tub below, and is great to lean against as you ogle the view of the tub room. The ceiling slopes at the back of the loft, which is cozy and attic-like. The room beneath has a bunk-bed quality with a view over the submerged hot tub and through the window wall. This space and the loft nook can be closed off with interior glass walls and doors, providing a thermal seal from the tub room without losing the open feeling.

The entire job communicates a sense of getting the very most out of an economy of means and space—a building tradition that never seems to go out of style.

The hot tub room in silhouette from the south-facing window wall. *Photo: Michael J. Crosbie.*

Detail of thermal mass and shower. *Photo: Michael J. Crosbie.*

Suburban Renewal
1982

Both John and Greg worked on the design of this house renovation near Princeton, New Jersey, but the result clearly reveals the younger's hand. Being of a different generation, his choice of materials and their use is certainly not rustic, a quality that Greg wanted to distance himself from a bit. "It's kind of magazine slick, but it's fun to do; to use some finer materials such as glass block and glazed tile."

Although this is not new construction, very little of the original house remains. "I touched every piece of that house," Greg says. The clients, Ali and Burgel Zomorodi, originally wanted a new gable roof to replace the leaky flat one on their 1950s house. But as the architects got into the job, rooting their way through rotted wood, it became clear that the place needed a total overhaul. At that point the Zomorodis decided to expand as well, and many of the rooms changed function in the process. "We tore the house up with the people living in it the whole time," says Greg, who is still amazed at the clients' patience and understanding as their house literally disappeared and reappeared before their eyes.

The exterior has a warm wood character. Natural pine soffits widen and narrow as they make

Dining alcove. *Photo: Greg Torchio.*

their way around the house, responding to drops and gaps that existed in the original roof— one of the biggest problems to deal with. "It had different levels because of the different additions," Greg explains. "We tried to get the whole thing coordinated with one fascia line all the way around. That's how we ended up with the big soffits." Pine is also used in the entry, which moved toward the street from its original position. A long exterior corridor now leads to it, also clad in pine. This corridor receives overhead natural light that slides down between the house and garage. The brown color for the redwood siding was chosen to hide the old color of red in one coat. On the south

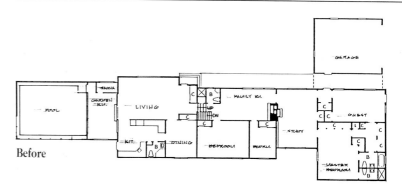

Before

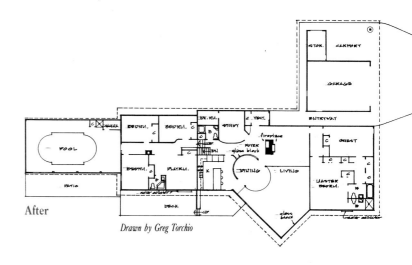

After

Drawn by Greg Torchio.

Sheathing the dining alcove. *Photo: Greg Torchio.*

South elevation shortly after completion. *Photo: Greg Torchio.*

Construction and sheathing of soffits. *Photo: Greg Torchio.*

Cornerstone planter built by Greg. *Photo: Greg Torchio.*

walls are a number of solar heat collectors designed and built by Jim that are made of black corrugated aluminum sheets behind pieces of patio door glass, vented at the top with tennis ball stops.

Inside, it's a bit slicker. Glass block is used to separate the kitchen and dining area while allowing light to pass through.

Compared to the voluminous, sunlit living room, the dining area is cozy; its ceiling drops down to make it so. The curved line of this drop ceiling is traced in the tile floor just below it, demarcating living from eating realms. The living room's tile is warmed by the sun coming through large, south-facing windows and light admitted by a clerestory that passes through the living room's gabled overhang. Glass block is

Curved glass block wall of dining alcove. *Photo: Greg Torchio.*

View toward living room from bedroom hallway. *Photo: Greg Torchio.*

also used in the hallway to shed light to a bedroom on the north side. In the pool room to the rear, prefabricated trusses are used to support a new, skylit roof. The trusses are pressure treated to reduce the chance of rot, as is the other wood used here. The south wall is a combination of wood frame windows and glass block.

Amid the glitter, however, are homages to the craftsman tradition. The kitchen sports cabinets made by outside craftsmen, but other details reveal Greg's skill. A study near the front entrance has a curved door that he built himself, as he did all the trim. The pool came in handy for soaking baseboard so that it would conveniently bend around some curved walls. In the hallway is a handmade railing that Greg crafted out of bits and pieces of

scrap pine exterior trim, and the patio furniture is another example of his handiwork. Be there any doubts that Jersey Devil has been this way, the attention to detail and the concrete footing near the entrance should put them to rest.

Custom built cabinets and south-facing kitchen window. *Photo: Greg Torchio.*

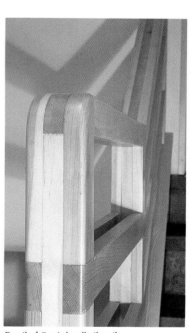

Detail of Greg's handbuilt rail.
Photo: Greg Torchio.

Music Room Addition
1983

As a counterpoint to Jersey Devil's usually bold statements, this music room addition to a house in Princeton, New Jersey, designed and built by John, is gentle and unassuming like its creator. Its reserved setting is appropriate for the performance of chamber music—the room's primary function. A garage once stood on the same spot and the first scenario was to refurbish it. But the structure was in such bad shape that it was demolished, leaving John a clean slate, and a pile of reusable material.

The addition's exterior has a distinctive Japanese presence. Approaching from the driveway, the sloped roof follows the curve of the wall below it, which pulls back, allowing you to pass between it and a tall pine tree to make your way to the entrance. The vertical siding is tongue and groove pine that has weathered to a light gray and stops just short of the ground, apparently floating on its black base. Above your head, the roof appears to defy gravity as well. "Up to the last minute I wasn't sure I could support it without a column," says John, adding that there is a

Framing in the cantilevered roof. *Photo: John Ringel.*

South-facing windows with clerestories. *Photo: John Ringel.*

Detail of entry overhang. *Photo: John Ringel.*

lot of hidden framing the building inspector suggested was a shame to hide. The soffit is sheathed in beaded, tongue and groove paneling that John salvaged from the demolished garage.

Up the slate and pebble walk and through the door, you arrive in a small foyer with a handbuilt shelf that proudly displays all its nails. John intended it to be painted but the client liked its natural state. Around the corner the music room unfolds, naturally lit with south-facing windows and skylights in the roof. Deciduous trees minimize summer sun and admit winter sun, its warmth absorbed by the room's black slate floor.

Drawn by John Ringel

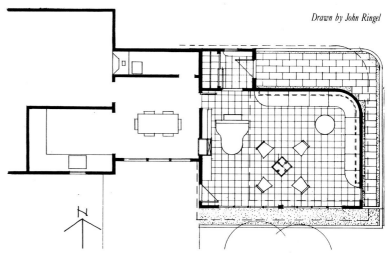

Framing over entryway. Photo: John Ringel.

At first the room appears to be a variation on a theme of gray and white walls, but here's another illusion. All the walls are white, their gray appearance due to their reflection of ambient light. The curve of the room is reinforced by a floating cornice that traverses the wall but doesn't appear to touch it. It is actually held away from the wall by plexiglass brackets and its height ghosts the roof cornice outside. Illuminated from behind, the cornice bathes the curved wall in soft light.

On the other side of the room is a gray, handbuilt cabinet, framed on one side by a door to a patio and on the other by an entrance to the dining room, in which John built another cabinet, back to back. The ceiling drops down above the music room cabinet where a piano is placed, designating a performance area.

The clients report that the room has excellent acoustics and this is matched by its quiet architecture. As John describes the room: "It doesn't necessarily stand out, but there's care, and I think people notice care. They recognize when something has been thoughtfully put together."

Performance alcove with handbuilt cabinets behind. *Photo: John Ringel.*

Cornice as it follows curve of wall. *Photo: John Ringel.*

". . . with a little help from our friends."

Over the years many people have worked with Jersey Devil in constructing the projects. They are noted here, with thanks.

Snail House (Steve and John): Patrick "Block" Bushnell, Joe "The Trowel" Lombardo, Rosemarie Lo Presti, Craig Yanta, Forked River Diner.

Barrel Deck (Steve and John): Miriam Belov, Pat Bushnell, Tom Reynold's belt.

Stone House Renovation (Steve and John): Lisa Halaby, Owen Hooley, John Kemp (doors and upholstery), Pat Patterson.

Helmet House (Steve and John): Nash Glynn, Owen Hooley, Eloise LaGrone, Eve Ringel, Hugh Swift.

Silo House (Steve, John, and Jim): Pat Bushnell, Tom Galbraith, Owen Hooley, Kerry Keane, John Kemp, Josh Lipton, Steve Swift, Jamie Wyper, Craig Yanta.

Football House (Steve and Jim): Pat Patterson, Dency Rue.

Hill House (Steve and Jim): Chris Becker, Terry and Pete Brown (plumbing), Alison Cornwell (stone and glass masonry), Ron Day (cabinetry, master bedroom bed/vanity), Jim Dempsey (excavating, boulder work),

Monte Edelstein (exterior doors and general carpentry), Ron Emerson (stone and glass masonry, landscaping), Doug Hall, Peter Howell, Doug Hurr (stonework), Jeff Hurr (stonework), Tom Keller (kitchen cabinetry), Chip Lord, Pete Mercado (tile work), Glenn Nelson (structural consultant), Carol Norton, Ted Norton, Pat Patterson, Jody Proctor, Maria Ruiz (stonework), Paul Ryan, Tom Sargent (cabinetry, master bedroom bed/vanity), Curtis Schreier (interior doors and windmill foreman), Donna Walter (carvings, general carpentry), Lindsay Wasserman, Tom Webb (slab).

Airplane House (Steve and Jim): Alan and Scott Duftie (excavating), Larry Johnson, Lepley Plumbing, Dennis Maroney (structural consultant), Donna Walter.

L.A. Deck (Steve and Jim): Donco (stucco), Jack Jarmon, Pat Patterson, Donna Walter.

Lake of the Woods Deck (Steve): Tom Ashcraft, Edgar Marquardt, Tom Sargent, Donna Walter.

Hot Tub House (John and Greg): Brian Goodale, J. B. Hoff & Son (plumbing), Leroy Porter, Mark Richards, Bill Schnable (electric), Norm Torkelson, Rich Torkelson, Dave and Sandy.

Suburban Renewal (John and Greg): Cooper Drywall, Ever Ready Refrigeration (HVAC), J. B. Hoff & Son (plumbing), Roy Van Horn, Owen Hooley, Richard Jankiewicz, Greg Kyde, Bruce Leclair, Bob Lynch, Paradigm Inc. (kitchen), Bill Schnable (electric), Sundrive Inc. (roof), Westwood Tile, Grandpa Winkler (landscaping), Ali and Burgel Zomorodi (painting, misc.), Steve and Jim.

Music Room Addition (John): Connie's eye and Lee's ear, Ever Ready Refrigeration

(HVAC), Owen Hooley, Greg Kyde, Bob Lynch, Leroy Porter, Bill Schnable (electric), Rich Torkelson, Greg.

Hoagie House (Steve, John, Jim, and Greg): Advance Engineers (structural consultants), Tom Ashcraft, Eva Asztalos, Tony Bosecker, Joachim Bruchhauser, Bob Burke (plumbing), Capital Steel and Elton Iron, Howard Dautry (electric), Brian Ford (mechanical consultant), Joe

Gass (excavating), Kristina Hansson, Kevin and Larry Johnson, JSL Concrete, Lauren Maccoll, Jimmy McLean, Edgar Marquardt, Roger Cline's Master Metalworks (roofing), Annie Mathews, Mike and Christine Millan (Gate House kitchen), Pat Patterson, Tom Payne (HVAC), Bruce Reed and the Reverend (roofing), Tom Sargent, Joel Siebentritt, Mark Three Stars, Donna Walter, John Walter (fireplace), Mike Walter.

Photo: Mary Lou Swift.

Acknowledgments

I would like to thank the members of Jersey Devil for their support and help with this book, especially their text reviews and suggestions. I also appreciate their patience and insight during my interviews with them, without which their story could not be told.

To my colleagues and friends at *Architecture* magazine, my thanks for their encouragement and good humor. To the clients of Jersey Devil's projects, thanks for allowing me to visit their homes. Gratitude to those who contributed their photographs include Peter Aaron, Allen Freemen, Bob Moore, and Max White. Essential for their photographic assistance were Sheryl Romeo and Peter O. Whiteley. I also want to thank Gibbs M. Smith for indulging a neophyte book writer and Roberta Vellvé at Peregrine Smith for her sensitive editing.

To Forrest Wilson I express my thanks for his insightful foreword. As my teacher and friend, his influence led to my writing such a book in the first place and without him it would have certainly taken a different point of view.

Finally, to Sharon, I want to share my gratitude for her patient understanding, encouragement, traveling companionship, and professional appraisals of this venture.

Author's Note

Michael J. Crosbie is a native of Dover, New Jersey. He studied architecture at Catholic University where he earned a Bachelors, Masters, and Ph.D. While a student he served as a design studio critic and received the American Institute of Architects'

Henry Adams Medal and Certificate for excellence in the study of architecture. He now teaches architectural journalism at Catholic University. Dr. Crosbie has done research on the effect of early industrialization on the architectural profession, industrialized building for housing, and owner-homebuilding and improvement. He is currently associate editor of *Architecture* magazine and has written on various architectural subjects, such as interiors, renovation and adaptive use, energy-conscious design, housing, technology, and education. He has worked in the building trade as a painter and lives in Washington, D.C.

Michael J. Crosbie. *Photo: Allen Freeman.*